D0245837

CHERYL
COLE

CHERYL COLE

Her Story – The Unauthorized Biography

GERARD SANDERSON

MICHAEL O'MARA BOOKS LIMITED

First published in Great Britain in 2008 by
Michael O'Mara Books Limited
9 Lion Yard
Tremadoc Road
London SW4 7NQ

Revised and updated paperback edition first published in 2009

A CIP catalogue record for this book is available from the British Library.

Papers used by Michael O'Mara Books Limited are natural, recyclable
products made from wood grown in sustainable forests. The
manufacturing processes conform to the environmental regulations
of the country of origin.

ISBN: 978-1-84317-389-2

5 7 9 10 8 6 4

Designed and typeset by E-Type

Plate section designed by Ana Bjezancevic

Printed and bound in Great Britain by Cox & Wyman, Reading, Berks

www.mombooks.com

Contents

Acknowledgements

To MG, who has made life so much fun – long may it last!

To my mum, for everything she's done for me and for showing me how to do double spacing automatically.

To Cheryl Cole, for being witty, fabulous and making the world a much brighter place!

And thanks to everyone who helped me in writing this book!

Photograph Acknowledgements

Page 1: © AM Models (*top* and *bottom left*) / Courtesy of
Whitley Bay Pantomime Society (*bottom right*)

Page 2: Mirrorpix/*Newcastle Evening Chronicle*

Page 3: Mirrorpix/*Newcastle Evening Chronicle* (*both images*)

Page 4: Mirrorpix/*Newcastle Evening Chronicle* (*both images*)

Page 5: *Newcastle Evening Chronicle*/Mirrorpix (*main image*) / ITV/Rex Features (*inset*)

Page 6: ITV/Rex Features (*top*) / Getty Images (*bottom*)

Page 7: Ken McKay/Rex Features

Page 8: Rob Morrison/allaction.co.uk/EMPICS
Entertainment/PA Photos (*top*) / Ian West/PA
Archive/PA Photos (*bottom*)

Page 9: Mirrorpix (*top*) / Matthew Fearn/PA Archive/PA
Photos (*bottom*)

Page 10: Rob Cable/LFI (*top left* and *right*) / Justin Goff/UK
Press/PA Photos (*bottom*)

Page 11: Huw John/Rex Features (*top*) / Barry Clark/
LFI (*bottom left*) / cruisepictures/EMPICS
Entertainment/PA Photos (*bottom right*)

Page 12: Getty Images

Page 13: © 2007 Scoopt/Getty Images (*top left*) / Nils
Jorgensen/Rex Features (*top right*) / Getty Images
(*bottom*)

Page 14: Ken McKay/Rex Features (*top*) / Most Wanted/Rex Features (*bottom left*) / David Fisher/Rex Features (*bottom right*)

Page 15: Ken McKay/Rex Features (*both images*)

Page 16: Dave M. Benett/Getty Images (*top*) / Suzan/EMPICS Entertainment/PA Photos (*bottom*)

INTRODUCTION

As the black limo swept towards the entrance of Arsenal's Emirates Stadium, the paparazzi raised their cameras in feverish expectation, knowing that just the right shot of its occupant could result in a handsome pay cheque. Behind them, a gaggle of fans and wannabe popstars, who had turned out for the latest set of *The X Factor* auditions, bubbled with excitement, eager to lay eyes on the big name that was about to step out and greet them.

Inside the car, Girls Aloud singer Cheryl Cole could feel butterflies fill her tummy. Today, 12 June 2008, was a big day for her. It was her very first day on the set of the fifth series of the top-rated TV talent show and she was nervous. Which was most unlike her, because she was never normally the kind of girl to be affected by nerves. She was the ambitious, driven woman who had not only gone from living on a council estate in Newcastle to becoming a household name, but had also very recently performed to audiences of over 100,000 on the Girls Aloud tour without any hint of fear whatsoever.

Today was different, however. Today was a big deal for her, for many reasons. As well as this being her first proper TV gig without the security of her four bandmates around her, she knew the country's media would be watching her every move, because she was the one who had been chosen to replace the mighty Sharon Osbourne on *The X Factor* judging panel.

Ever since the flamboyant Sharon had sensationally quit the show earlier in the year amid rumours of financial quibbles and a much-publicized rift with fellow judge Dannii Minogue, speculation was rife about who would take her place. Outspoken Spice Girl Mel B was in the frame for a time, so too was Amanda Holden. But it was Cheryl Cole who turned out to be the clear favourite, particularly after her profile had shot through the roof back in February, when allegations hit the tabloids that her husband Ashley had been less than faithful.

Cheryl had initially been a little hesitant about accepting the role. After all, she'd been through this arduous audition process herself during *Popstars: The Rivals* and knew first hand the effect the judges' tough comments could have on a naïve wannabe with a head full of dreams. Could she be responsible for shattering the hopes of these fragile young people? She wasn't sure. 'Who am I to judge other people?' she confessed in an ITV press release in 2007, when it was rumoured that she was to join ITV's *Britain's Got Talent* judging team. 'I know people think I am fiery but I think I'm too diplomatic. I know what it's like to be on the receiving end of criticism.' But surely, to turn down a TV job as prestigious as *The X Factor* would have been seen as madness? She had to take the job, didn't she?

Cheryl could take heart from Sharon Osbourne's effusive recommendation of her for the role on Chris Moyles' BBC Radio 1 show: 'I think Cheryl would be perfect for the job,' she gushed. 'She will take the show in another direction.' John Kaye Cooper,

ITV's Controller of Entertainment, added his praise in an ITV press release, stating that: 'Cheryl is not only an amazingly successful, sassy and talented woman but through her winning *Popstars: The Rivals* she has been through similar experiences to those hopefuls who want to take *The X Factor* crown.'

And so, once the car had pulled up to the entrance, she stepped out, finally feeling confident and assured, and gave the paparazzi her killer Cole smile as they shot a rapid machine-gun fire of camera flashes. As Cheryl strode into the arena to start her brand new job of judging the country's talent, the irony was not wasted on her: her life had come full circle, and six years after she'd been discovered on a talent show, she was back again – only this time, she was in control . . .

Chapter 1
BONNIE BABIES

Even as a six-year-old, Cheryl Ann Tweedy knew that she was destined to follow a path that would take her a world away from her run-down neighbourhood of Heaton in Newcastle. Too young to understand what it meant to hold down a nine-to-five job or indeed the reasons why it was important actually to have one, Cheryl was dreaming of a more glamorous life as a world-famous star.

And on a sunny day in 1990, her dreams would seem not to be so far-fetched after all. Standing in front of a team of stern-looking judges in the centre of Newcastle in a frilly skirt and flowery blouse, the pretty little girl with bouncy pigtails stood with thirteen other young hopefuls, quaking in their tiny shoes as they waited to discover which of them would be named 'Star of the Future' by local newspaper the *Evening Chronicle*.

Although the competition was just a bit of fun for the local children to get involved in, those taking part took it all very seriously indeed; in particular young Cheryl, who, having won numerous talent and beauty prizes over the years, did not want her winning streak to end. Even at such a young age, Cheryl was remarkably confident and self-assured, and she knew from her previous successes that she had that certain something that made people instantly fall in love with her. She thrived on performing and being the centre of attention, but then, being the fourth of five children, this was hardly surprising. 'I had to stand out somehow,' Cheryl said in ITV2's 2008 documentary *The Passions of Girls Aloud*. 'So I used to love dancing and just generally showing off.'

However, in spite of her impressive self-confidence, this plucky little star-in-the-making knew that nothing was ever a certainty, that every competition was different and that she might not always come away with the prize. And this citywide competition was particularly tough. Although she knew she had done her best by demonstrating her natural dancing abilities, she was aware that the decision was not in her power. It was now up to a panel of judges to decide which of the fourteen youngsters they believed had the potential to go on and become a massive star in the future.

When Mike Whitehouse, competition judge and store manager of local clothes chain and contest sponsor Children's World, finally stepped up to put the ensemble of kiddies out of their misery, Cheryl could feel her heart beating heavily in her chest. However, to those around her, she apparently looked remarkably calm and, as some who took part on the day have said since, oozed an unfathomable confidence.

As she waited for Mike to deliver his verdict, Cheryl looked over at her mother Joan, who was sitting on the edge of her seat in the audience, beaming with pride. Whatever the result,

Cheryl knew that her mother would be proud of her. Joan could never be described as a pushy mother. She'd simply spotted a seed of talent and star quality in her daughter and had sown it straight away; in other words, responded to her ambitious daughter's creative leanings . . .

As soon as Cheryl was born on 20 June 1983, Joan knew that her second daughter was different from her other children, Joseph, Andrew and Gillian. Although she couldn't put her finger on it straight away, she could sense that Cheryl had a unique quality that made her stand out. It was also fortunate that the wee girl happened to be very easy on the eye. 'Cute as a button,' a friend of the family told Newcastle's *Chronicle* newspaper. 'Such a pretty little girl, who would turn heads wherever she went.'

So on the advice of family friends, and before Cheryl was even able to crawl, Joan introduced her daughter to the world of showbiz by entering her into a number of 'Bonnie Baby' competitions. And her decision proved to be a canny one. When she entered Cheryl for the 'Boots The Chemist's Bonniest Baby' contest, her little cherub was easily named the winner. The result was the same when Cheryl took part in the 'Mothercare's Happy Faces' contest and again when she was a contestant in the *Evening Chronicle*'s 'Little Miss and Mister' competition.

Joan's belief that her daughter was special appeared not just to be feelings of maternal pride; judging committees all across Newcastle had agreed with her. And by naming her little one winner of their contests, the message was loud and clear – Cheryl Ann Tweedy was a girl to watch out for!

Of course, all this success meant that back at Casa Tweedy –

a narrow and rather modest three-storey council house in the run-down Heaton district – the family's living-room cabinet was positively straining under the weight of Cheryl's prize statuettes. And Cheryl's continued streak of success meant that housewife Joan and her partner Garry knew that their daughter had a talent that had to be nurtured, even if it meant having to scrimp and save to ensure she was able to attend auditions.

'There wasn't a lot of money, but Mum and Dad always found enough for my audition outfits,' Cheryl recalled about the early days of her career in the *Mirror*. 'My mum would take me to auditions. If I got a part, Dad would shout, "Get in there!" like a football fan but all Mum would say was, "Oh good." She will always keep my feet on the ground.'

But it wasn't long before Cheryl's talent and cute looks enabled her to earn back some of the money her parents had invested in her. A friend of Joan's suggested that perhaps Cheryl, who by then was just four years old, should join a modelling agency. Spurred on by her friend's comments and the well-polished trophies that sparkled at home, Joan signed her daughter up to an agency run by Pat Morgan. And the union proved fruitful, as Joan recalls: 'She did loads for the Pat Morgan Agency from the age of four, and went to shopping centres all over the place, strutting her stuff on the catwalks and stages.' So, even at this young age, Cheryl was already on her way to stardom, albeit locally for now.

As Mike Whitehouse cleared his throat to announce the winner of the *Evening Chronicle*'s 'Star of the Future', Cheryl sized up her competition. Had any of the other children, such as Alexander Bensley or Ryan Silmon or Clare Allan or Claire Swinney, managed to outshine her that afternoon?

She certainly hoped not! She'd put on a good show, she knew that, and she'd flashed the judges her brightest smile. And she looked good, too. Cheryl's mum had bought her the sassiest outfit their money could buy, and her hair had been twisted into two heart-meltingly cute pony tails. Surely she had the prize – £150 worth of Children's World vouchers – in the bag.

And so, the moment had arrived when one of the expectant children would become the happiest in all of Newcastle. 'Thank you all for coming today,' Whitehouse began. 'It's been a wonderful day, but of course there can only be one winner . . .' Cheryl glanced at her mum one last time and conjured up her best Oscars-worthy smile so that, if her name wasn't the one called, she wouldn't look too disappointed. 'And the winner is . . .' Mike paused for dramatic effect. 'Cheryl Tweedy.'

It took a couple of seconds for the words to sink in, but when they did, the little six-year-old erupted into squeals of joy. Her mother dashed towards her and wrapped her up in her arms. Cheryl had won yet again. It looked as if there was absolutely no stopping her. Nor was there any stopping her when it came to using those gift vouchers she had won as a prize. 'It was a lovely day,' her mum said of Cheryl's triumph in the *Evening Chronicle*. 'She really enjoyed herself. As a kid, that was her thing – dressing up and putting on a show. She has always been into clothes and when she won those vouchers she was thrilled because she could buy more.'

But that honour was far from the end of Cheryl's glories. Not long afterwards, she was awarded the top prize in the 'Best Looking Girl in Newcastle' contest and – as if she hadn't already won enough awards – was also named the 'Most Attractive Girl' at Gateshead's Metro Centre (the largest shopping and leisure complex in Europe).

Ambitious Cheryl wasn't content with just winning beauty contests, however: she wanted to be a star. When she was seven, she finally got the break into TV that she'd been waiting for, when she landed an acting gig with kid brother Garry in an advert for British Gas. In the thirty-second clip, a naked Cheryl is seen being bathed in a bath full of bubbles with her brother. Although the ad could potentially be slightly embarrassing when viewed years later, Cheryl's mum said in the *Daily Star* that this wasn't the case for her daughter. 'She isn't really embarrassed about it because she was just a little girl. It proved she was a natural in front of the cameras.'

Shortly afterwards, the Tweedy twosome were hired once again to appear in an advert for Newcastle's Eldon Square shopping centre. Cheryl's award-winning dark eyes and prize-winning gorgeous face had captivated the folks of Newcastle, and it wasn't long before she was being asked to appear in yet another advert, this time for Sunderland-based furniture retailer SCS – even if it did mean she had to wear a rather garish mid-nineties rainbow-coloured waistcoat!

While the youngster was enjoying every opportunity that came her way, ambitious Cheryl didn't just want to live off her looks. She had a dream and she was determined to make it come true: she wanted to dance. But, as she would soon find out, sometimes dreams don't always turn out quite as you'd imagined.

Chapter 2
DANCING QUEEN

Ever since she could walk, young Cheryl Tweedy had demonstrated a keen interest in dancing. Whenever she could, she would sneak off to her bedroom, turn on some music and work out her own routines.

'I'd shut the door, play my songs and pretend I was in a video,' she remembered in the ITV2 documentary series *The Passions of Girls Aloud*. 'But I would always get caught in the middle of a dance move, and I'd be so embarrassed, because my older brothers and sister would take the mick out of me and say stuff like "We were spying on you".'

Cheryl didn't care, however. She knew she had rhythm, and she knew that she *really* enjoyed dancing. Although she was happy enough twirling, spinning and gyrating to the latest pop tunes on the radio, secretly, Cheryl harboured a burning desire to slip on a tutu and become a ballerina. What little ballet she had already seen had been enough to mesmerize her. The beautiful, graceful moves of the dancers were hypnotic and she longed to be on stage performing pirouettes herself. Like most girls, Cheryl saw ballet as something magical. There was something so fragile and sophisticated about the way a ballerina glided across the floor. And she knew in her heart that she could do the same if only she were given the chance.

Recognizing that her daughter had a gift, mum Joan took Cheryl along to ballet lessons at the Margaret Waite School of Dancing in Whitley Bay, where Cheryl proved to be something of a hit. Even though she was one of many enthusiastic youngsters with a hopeful glint in their eye, it was Cheryl who stood out. She flew across the floor like a leaf on a breeze, and her lightness of step and ability to move to the music was immediately noted by Margaret, who declared that Cheryl was 'an exceptional dancer'. As any mother would be, Joan was thrilled that her little girl's dreams seemed about to come true; that her daughter was lucky enough not only to have the ambition and drive to succeed, but more rarely, the skill to match them. As Joan recalled on *The Passions of Girls Aloud*: 'In her first lesson, the teacher took me aside and said that Cheryl had something special.'

With her expert knack for picking up routines almost immediately, it wasn't long before Cheryl was being given parts in local shows. One of the highlights was a small role in the Whitley Bay Pantomime Society's production of *Aladdin*. Despite only having a minor part, Cheryl saw her participation as a way to shine in front of an audience, which she relished. It may have been a far cry from London's West End, but the Whitley Bay Pantomime Society provided yet another opportunity for her to dazzle in front of an audience.

Impressed by Cheryl's stage presence and technical ability, Margaret suggested that perhaps her little nine-year-old protégé ought to try for a place at the Royal Ballet's Summer School in London. Cheryl's eyes lit up immediately she heard this. The chance to go and study at the Royal Ballet in London? She just couldn't believe what she was hearing. Not only would this mean that she would be training with professional dancers who had performed in many world-famous productions, but she would also get the chance to see another part of the world other than her beloved Newcastle. The process wasn't easy: Cheryl had to take on five thousand other young, excited hopefuls. Luckily for her, however, the gods were on her side, and she made it through to the final selection with ease. She and her mum could not contain their excitement. Cheryl was going to London to dance with the Royal Ballet!

This was amazing news for the Tweedy family. After all, this kind of thing didn't happen to people like them. Dad Garry was a painter and decorator, while Mum was a housewife, and with five kids they sometimes struggled to make ends meet. One of their children dancing with the Royal Ballet seemed like a plot lifted straight out of a film. But this was real. The Royal Ballet had decided that Cheryl was good enough to travel to London to be taken under their wing and perhaps to become a star of the future.

Although she was used to winning 'Bonnie Baby' competitions and landing roles in adverts during her early years, Cheryl was convinced now that her life was about to turn a corner. If she did well during the fortnight-long Summer School there was every possibility that Cheryl would be asked to attend the Royal Ballet School full time. She knew that this was a once-in-a-lifetime opportunity and there was no way she was going to let it slip through her fingers.

What she hadn't realized, however, was the fact that, despite winning a place on the course, her parents were going to have to shell out £300 for the privilege. It was the early nineties, and the family were finding life relatively hard financially. While they were living a fairly comfortable life, having to spend such a large sum of money left Joan and Garry feeling anxious. There was just no way they could raise the cash for the course in time, but they both knew that there was no way in the world they could deny their eager young daughter the chance to fulfil her dream of dancing. So Cheryl's mum and dad made the tough decision to ask around for help. Although they were a proud couple who didn't believe in handouts, they knew that if their little girl was to be able to take advantage of this rare opportunity, they would have to try anything they could to make it happen.

And so Garry and Joan launched a fundraising campaign in their local area. As luck would have it, a sponsor came forward with the money. Cheryl and her family couldn't hide their joy and Cheryl was keen to thank the kind Samaritan. 'I want to thank them so much,' she told the *Evening Chronicle* at the time. 'I promise I will do my best.' Giddy with delight, her mum was just as pleased, as it meant that her daughter was finally going to be doing something she loved: 'It's fantastic that she's going to ballet school,' Joan said at the time to the *Chronicle*. 'It would have broken Cheryl's heart if she had missed out.'

At last, Cheryl was all set to conquer the world of ballet. Travelling down south was an exciting experience for the young Geordie lass. In her mind, London was the city she'd heard described by her elders; the place where the streets were paved in gold; where young people's dreams came true; where anyone could become a star. As she made her way to the school in London's leafy Richmond on her first day, she couldn't believe that she, Cheryl Ann Tweedy, was in the big smoke embarking on an adventure of a lifetime.

And when she laid eyes on the impressive White Lodge building, which was to be her home for the next two weeks, she was even more awestruck. Situated in the heart of the sumptuous Richmond Park, south-west London, the eighteenth-century building looked like the kind of grand pile Cheryl had seen in those Sunday afternoon BBC costume dramas. She couldn't believe her eyes when she saw the grand cream building looming above her. It looked like nothing she'd ever seen before in real life. Cheryl squeezed her mum's hand and the pair exchanged looks. This was it: the start of the rest of Cheryl's life. They felt a million miles from the world they both knew. Certainly it would be hard to go back to what she was used to after this. The next two weeks were going to be the best of her life, she felt sure of it. If she did well and was offered a place on the five-year course, she would not only get to study classical ballet, she'd also be taught gymnastics, and Irish, Scottish and Morris dancing, while later on in the course she'd be schooled in repertoire, solos and *pas de deux*.

Of course, there was a downside. In conjunction with the dance aspects of the course, Cheryl, if she were to be accepted, would have to study academic subjects, too, such as Maths and English. But as long as she could dance, she didn't really mind if she had to squeeze in a bit of swotting. So the next fourteen days, Cheryl knew, were crucial. If she did well, a door would be opened and life would never be the same again.

Sadly, her experience on the course was not to live up to her expectations. The moment she stepped into the studio for the first time and looked around at the other children, Cheryl felt she didn't belong and that the life she had dreamed about for so long was perhaps not for her after all. For one, none of the other children or parents appeared to be too friendly and they all kept themselves to themselves. For another, Cheryl thought they seemed a little snobbish for her liking, appearing to look down their noses at her. There was a divide for sure: while she and Joan were dressed in their mid-price clothes from home, the other children's parents were decked out in designer gear and seemed to walk around as if they owned the place.

London was certainly different to Newcastle, but the cultural and class gulf between Cheryl and the other children was even more immense. She had so wanted to enjoy her experience in London and the chance to learn and get to know some new and like-minded people, but it just wasn't to be. Over the course of the next fortnight, miles away from her family and friends, she became increasingly introverted. She felt alone, out of place and homesick.

'I wanted to go home straight away,' she said years later in the *Daily Mirror*. 'Everyone was prim and proper and I was just a Geordie from a council estate. The parents all had money and we struggled just to get cash to travel down to London. I felt that I was the odd one out.'

In spite of her insecurities, however, she didn't let her isolation put her off what she was there to do, and she excelled in her classes on the course. She realized, too, that no amount of money could replace the strength of the bond she had with her devoted mother Joan. When parents were invited along to see their children's final performance, Cheryl told the *Mirror* she was the only one who acknowledged her mother.

After the final performance, Cheryl made a decision that she never thought she'd make: she was turning her back on ballet once and for all. The homesickness she'd suffered, the teary nights she'd spent tucked up in bed and the lack of camaraderie between the pupils had left her feeling very disillusioned, and her plans to be a professional ballerina who danced on stages around the world were forgotten there and then. 'It shattered my dream,' she admitted in the *Daily Mirror* interview, looking back. 'But I didn't want to have to stand a certain way all my life and only eat salad.'

Thankfully, this particular experience didn't put her off dancing altogether. Back in Newcastle she attended the Newcastle Dance Centre, where she excelled at a wide range of dance styles. Her skill was of such a high calibre that she went on to win numerous dance competitions. Eventually, she teamed up with a boy from the centre for the British Dance Championships, and the pair of them appeared on Michael Barrymore's successful TV show *My Kind of People*. But that wasn't their only taste of TV stardom. They also appeared on the Saturday morning kids' show *Gimme 5* and enjoyed enough screen time to have their friends back at the centre and at school agog with excitement. It was also clear to Cheryl that performing in front of the cameras came naturally to her. Little did she know then that it would stand her in good stead in the future when she'd take part in a TV show called *Popstars: The Rivals*.

Chapter 3
PLAYGROUNDS AND PARTYING

By the time she was a teenager, it seemed clear that Cheryl Tweedy was destined to become a star, but that didn't mean her life was all song and dance. In fact, when she wasn't singing into her hairbrush or bopping away to the hits of boyband Five, she was just like most teenage girls who passed the time hanging out with her friends, larking about with boys and watching chick flicks such as *Grease*, *Ghost* and *Dirty Dancing* so many times that she could probably reel off the scripts word for word if she were asked to.

In spite of her lofty ambitions, family life with her three brothers and one sister was pretty run-of-the-mill. All of them were given chores to do and taught to look out for each other. Life in their cramped house wasn't exactly like an episode of the *The Waltons*, however. Far from it. The kids could be little terrors and often ran rampant around the house, proving to be something of a handful for poor Joan and Garry. 'Our neighbours must have hated us,' Cheryl confided on *Loose Women* years later. 'We were such a noisy bunch of kids.' Joseph, the eldest, was born in 1976, Gillian came next in 1979, and Andrew followed in 1980. When Cheryl came along in the summer of 1983, four years before youngest brother Garry, the boisterous young Tweedys had found a brand new toy to play with in their little sister. And play with her they did, as Cheryl recalled in an interview with *Top of the Pops* magazine in 2003. 'I learnt how to fight cos me brothers would joke about and hang me over balconies. I had to learn self-defence.'

Although Joan spent much of her time tending to Cheryl's creative needs, she also had to make sure that the rest of the children didn't feel neglected. As a busy housewife, Joan had to make sure that she found time for each of her kids. Having had her first child at just seventeen, the youthful mother had formed a close bond with her children.

'She had to grow up fast,' Cheryl said of her mum in the *Daily Mirror*. 'And with five of us she had to work hard.' Life certainly wasn't easy, and Joan struggled, but with strength, determination and the love and support of her family, she managed to muddle through the rough times. 'Dad supported all of us because my mum wanted to bring us up well.'

Money may have been tight but Joan and Garry made sure that the children were well looked after. 'There were five of us, so there wasn't much money,' Cheryl told *Top of the Pops* magazine. 'We weren't spoilt at all.'

Christmases were family orientated, though never very ostentatious. However, although they were on a budget, it didn't mean festive times at the Tweedys weren't fun. One particular Christmas Day, Cheryl and her siblings woke up bright and early to see what was waiting for them under the tree. Instead of finding a delightful pile of shiny gifts, however, they found a mass of shredded wrapping paper strewn across the floor and their presents tossed around the room. For a moment, the little ones thought that local tearaways had crept into their house during the night to cause havoc. But when their pet pooch Monty strolled up to them sheepishly, it dawned on them that perhaps the culprit was actually a little closer to home. 'He'd chewed off the paper and then he got told off by mum,' Cheryl remembered in the *Top of the Pops* magazine. 'I think he was looking for his own present – some bones. Monty was mental; the baubles on the Christmas tree just sent him mad.'

Home life might have been chaotic at times but it was a loving household, and gave Cheryl the stability she needed to be able to go off and enjoy school. By her own admission, Cheryl wasn't the most academic of kids at Walker Comprehensive School in Newcastle. But as far as grades were concerned, she was an adequate scholar. This might have had something to do with the fact that it wasn't always her own work that she'd hand in to the teacher. Busy being popular at school meant Cheryl didn't always have the time to concentrate on finishing her work, so occasionally she'd have to use nefarious means to gain the adequate grades. 'I used to look at other people's books and copy them,' she confessed to *Top of the Pops*. 'I didn't get caught, though, because I was crafty. The geeks used to try to hide their work but I was friendly to them so they didn't mind.'

If she had applied herself better at school, she might have ended up in an entirely different line of work: 'If I'd had a sensible head on my shoulders when I was at school I'd have loved to have gone into forensic detective work,' she revealed during an interview on Real Radio. 'I'd have loved it. I find it fascinating, like which way the blood is splattered and stuff.' However, in spite of her rather dubious methods of gaining good marks, Cheryl made a good impression on the teachers at Walker's. Dr Steve Gater, the school principal at the time, remembered Cheryl fondly in the *Mirror* as a shining light and claimed to have recognized her potential straight away. 'It was obvious early on that Cheryl was ambitious and talented,' he said. 'From a young age her passions were singing and dancing. The staff didn't anticipate how big she would become but clearly the potential was there.'

He also remembered her as a confident young girl who was never too shy to command a crowd. 'She loved being centre stage. She stood head and shoulders above everybody else. Once she gave a speech to two hundred and fifty kids for a Christmas Box appeal and was so good that a letter of commendation was sent to her parents.'

However, Cheryl remembers her schooling a little bit differently. 'On my reports, it would say "Cheryl has great ability, she's capable of doing everything, but she'd prefer to talk to her friends."' She later told Barbara Ellen in *The Observer* that her naughty behaviour and lack of interest was such that she'd end up being punished rather severely. 'I was awful at school,' she declared. 'They used to throw me out of the classroom. My headmaster once said to me: "It'll be interesting to see what you do in your life, Miss Tweedy."'

And it would seem that Steve Gater has kindly overlooked the times when the tempestuous Cheryl was suspended from school for getting into a couple of spats with boys. As she would prove later, the determined little lass was certainly no pushover and if she felt she was being wronged then she'd stand up for herself. 'I got into a fight with a guy at school,' she told *Top of the Pops* magazine in 2003. 'He spat at me so I slapped him and we ended up both getting suspended.' But that wasn't her only brush with school authorities. She also landed herself in trouble when she had a squabble with a fellow pupil on her way home after school: 'I got suspended for two weeks for having an argument on a bus and using bad language. Someone on the bus told the school. He'd kicked me in the leg so I started arguing. He didn't get in trouble – I wasn't impressed.'

When she wasn't hammering it out with the boys, Cheryl spent her time getting friendly with them. With her striking looks and wicked sense of humour, she was never short of admirers in and around school, and Cheryl always made sure she never had to make do with second best. She was able to land herself top-of-the-range school hunks to go on dates with. The relationships at school never lasted very long and she admitted that she actually preferred spending time with her girlie mates – and her mum.

'My mam is a bigger clubber than me,' Cheryl once boasted to *Top of the Pops* magazine. 'She's a real trendy mum. She drags me on the dancefloor and doesn't stop; she'd dance on the sofas if she got the chance.'

But then Cheryl never really saw her mum as a mother figure. After all, the age gap wasn't huge and the pair were pretty inseparable. 'She is more like a friend,' she said. 'I can talk to her about anything – boyfriends, sex, you name it.'

However, this didn't mean that Joan let Cheryl run wild. Even though they were like sisters, Joan still made sure that rules were set in place. Joan made it clear that there were limits to what Cheryl could and couldn't do. She wasn't allowed to have boys stay over, nor was she allowed to go out gallivanting into the wee hours. Rebellious Cheryl wasn't having any of it. She wanted to party and have some fun, and she wasn't going to let rules stop her.

So, the canny lass used the usual teenage tricks so that she could meet up with her mates without her mother ever knowing. When she used to tell her mum that she was heading over to her friend Lindsay's house for a sleepover, she'd actually meet up with a gang of girls and boys and enjoy a night out under the stars. 'When I was about sixteen, I used to go camp out with my friends,' she recalled in *Top of the Pops*. 'There was a tent full of boys and a tent full of girls and I'd tell my mum I'd gone to stay at Lindsay's. 'She'd be like, "All right, love, see you in the morning!" I'd come back the next day like an ice block and be like, "Lindsay's mum's got no heating."'

But her mum soon wised up to what was going on when she finally caught Cheryl in the act. Most times when a pal came to stay, Cheryl would say goodnight to the family, then lead her friend upstairs to her bedroom, where they'd slip out of their pyjamas and into T-shirts and trackie bottoms ready to hit the town. Just in case Cheryl's mum came to check on them before she went to bed, the pair would climb into bed and pull the blankets up around their necks so it looked as if they were sleeping. Then at around 2 a.m., when the rest of the household was fast asleep, a bunch of boys would quietly stroll up to the house and throw something at the window to alert the girls of their arrival. The naughty pair would then spring out of bed, creep through the house and dash off for a fun night out.

And most of the time, they managed to get away with it without detection. But on one occasion, their wily ways were scuppered when they were stopped suddenly in their tracks by Joan, who had heard the commotion outside. Catching them, she blew her top, as Cheryl remembered in an interview with *Top of the Pops* magazine: 'She went mad – and nearly tore my head off my shoulders.'

Not all the male attention she received was desired, however. When she was fifteen to sixteen years old, Cheryl had a part-time job waitressing at a café called JJ's. Though she was still at school, she'd taken the job to earn a little extra cash so that she could buy some new clothes for the singing gigs she had started taking in the evenings around Newcastle. Thanks to her dazzling smile and chirpy banter, Cheryl proved a popular worker with customers and as a result managed to make good tips. But one particular customer made her feel a little uncomfortable when he started to pay her a lot more attention than she liked. At first, the thirty-something man had seemed perfectly nice, though certainly not the kind of man Cheryl would have found attractive herself. Nevertheless, she'd flash him a bright grin and engage him in conversation, just as she did all the customers. But there was something different about this man, something strange.

'He was fine at first,' she recalled in an interview with *Q* magazine, 'but then he started asking to look at my feet. I wore open-toed sandals and he said he loved my feet. He was about thirty years old and was sweaty and had spit in the corner of his mouth. I ran home and my brother came out to find him. He would have killed him!'

Fortunately other men would come into Cheryl's life who

proved to be considerably more eligible. But as it would turn out, those relationships were never going to be easy to maintain, particularly when stardom beckoned.

Chapter 4
BAD BOYS AND ROMANCE

Throughout her teens, gorgeous Cheryl had never been short of attention. During her school years she had dated the best-looking boys around. However, not many of her relationships were fulfilling – and she wasn't the kind of girl who was willing to let guys take her for a ride.

Not all boys were total wastes of space, however. Some, she felt, were worth taking a chance on . . . for a time, anyway! One of them was plumber Steve Thornton, whom she met when she was sixteen. In an interview with the *News of the World*, he claimed that the couple had enjoyed an intense relationship after meeting at the café she was working in.

'I was only there to collect my mates' breakfast on the building site,' he recalled. 'But I knew that I was on to something when she slipped in some extra rashers and handed them over with a really knowing look.' He went on to explain that the minute he saw her he thought she had the 'face of an angel' and that she was 'always smiling'. He claimed that she flirted with him outrageously over the counter. Not that he minded. 'I dreamed of kissing her,' he said, 'and after spending a fortune on sandwiches I finally got to take her out.'

Their first date wasn't the most romantic – a quick coffee at a local café – but they both enjoyed it. The conversation was natural and easy, and Steve knew there and then that Cheryl was potential girlfriend material. After the coffee, Cheryl invited him back to her sister Gillian's place to watch some TV. If Steve thought 'watching TV' was code for something else, he was sadly mistaken. 'It wasn't the most extravagant of first dates,' he told the *News of the World*. 'But when I kissed her at the end of the night everything seemed perfect.'

A simple beginning, but there was a definite spark between them and it wasn't long before the pair started dating, enjoying nights on the town or kissing and holding hands on Gillian's couch. Although they were taking things slowly, Steve claimed that frisky Cheryl would suggest what she'd like them to get up to, such as her dressing up as Britney, or slipping into a cowgirl's outfit on one occasion. The relationship lasted around five months before going cold and Cheryl apparently stopped taking his calls.

Steve revealed to the *News of the World* that he was heartbroken by Cheryl's decision. Eventually he moved on with his life, but in 2002 all the memories came flooding back when he saw Cheryl appear in the audition shows for *Popstars: The Rivals*. 'I was just sat at home on a Saturday night when they announced "Cheryl Tweedy from Newcastle". She looked just as lovely as I remember her. I always knew that she was something special, she always wanted to get to the top and it looks like now she is getting the chance to live her dream.'

Later, Cheryl admitted she was devastated when Steve sold his story to the newspaper. However, she said she took it on the chin, admitting, 'You just have to get a tougher skin, laugh it off.' When the story hit the stands, though, she was straight on the phone to find out why he had done this to her. 'I was so upset and so hurt,' she recalled. 'He treated me like shit the whole time I was seeing him. I rang him and said, "I want an explanation, because all I ever did was help and support you." He started crying and said the papers had been hounding him for ten months.'

Back in September 2000, however, a seventeen-year-old Cheryl met another boyfriend who would make a deep impact on her life. Strolling through the Byker region of Newcastle one afternoon after a shift at JJ's, she caught the eye of a furniture salesman called Jason Mack. 'From the moment I saw Cheryl I wanted her,' the shaven-headed shop assistant told the *News of the World*. 'She had the most perfect face, great legs and a fantastic backside.'

It wasn't long before they were dating seriously, but things weren't exactly easy-going. Cheryl's mum wasn't happy about her daughter spending too much time with Jason alone at his flat, and eventually suggested that he come and stay with them – a clever way to keep a keen eye on the pair of them. But as Joan would discover, she wasn't able to keep an eye on them all the time.

Whenever Joan went on her Saturday morning run to Morrisons, Jason claimed in the *News of the World* that he and Cheryl were able to indulge in bouts of passion. But when they weren't holed up in her room at home, they'd be out and about. Cheryl would treat Jason to expensive designer clothes, such as

Lacoste, Rockport and Henri Lloyd with money she had saved up from her wages from the café. In return he got himself a tattoo of a she-devil with the word 'Chez' etched underneath it.

But wise Joan had been right to keep an eye on Jason, as she would later find out that he had an ongoing problem with drugs and alcohol. In his *News of the World* interview, Jason revealed that when he first met Cheryl, he was 'doing a lot of cocaine' and on some days would 'blow £200 on the stuff'. He also admitted that as soon as he got up in the morning he'd be swigging from bottles of Bud until he 'crashed out at God knows when'.

Although Cheryl herself never indulged in such practices, Jason claimed that she was so besotted with him she couldn't turn her back on him and bravely tried to help him kick his nasty habit. It was tough, but she proved to be a patient and thoughtful counsellor who helped Jason through the worst of his problem. 'She'd sit with me for hours to talk me out of going out and getting drugs,' he confided. 'In a couple of weeks I turned my back on cocaine.'

Drugs were something that would play a major part in Cheryl's life over the next few years: their impact on her family and friends would have a lasting effect, ensuring that she'd never consider dabbling in any herself.

Living on a council estate in Heaton was hard for many of the youngsters. There was little money and even less for them to do.

'When I was growing up I did not have a clue about anything,' Cheryl said in *The New Statesman*. 'All I knew was going to school and going back to the council house, not always being able to have dinner, not knowing why we were skint, just assuming that's the way things had to be.'

And the solution for some of these directionless young people? To escape their monotonous lives by losing themselves in drugs. But Cheryl was different. Even though she'd quit school at sixteen, against her father's wishes, and was finding it hard to make ends meet with her café job, she was determined to make something of herself. Cheryl knew that she had something special and that she had a future in showbiz, and she sure as hell wasn't going to waste what talent she had, or any opportunities that came her way, by getting caught up in the world of drugs.

'Heroin was there for the taking,' she told *The Times* in 2007. 'I could easily have taken that route if I'd wanted to. But I always maintained my ambition and I'm proud of myself. That nightmare devastated family and friends, but I'm grateful. If I hadn't been exposed to that at such a young age, who knows what might have happened?'

But in 2005, Cheryl did experience what could have happened if she'd made the wrong decisions, when a school friend called John Courtney was found dead from a heroin overdose. The twenty-one-year-old had become friends with Cheryl during their time at Walker's School, and they had grown very close. Like Cheryl, John had dreams and potential. A gifted footballer, his sports teachers and the local football manager reckoned he had a bright future in the sport and dubbed him 'another Shearer'.

After leaving school, however, the good-natured boy's life was turned on its head when he became hooked on heroin and fell into a life of crime, which resulted in a jail spell. According to John's mum, Angie Courtney, Cheryl was a light in her son's life.

'She was always a lovely girl and a good friend of John's while they were teenagers,' she told local newspaper the *Evening Chronicle*. 'When John died, we got hundreds of flowers and more than three hundred cards, but hers were among the first to arrive. She sent them as soon as she heard. While John was alive, she came to our house and wrote him a note, telling him to get off the drugs and he kept it on his wall to remind him that he had to keep battling it.'

Sadly, Cheryl's attempts to help John shake off his habit failed, and on 2 April 2005, just three weeks after being released from prison, John's body was found curled up on a carpet in his uncle's house, a needle lying next to him. In order to raise awareness of the growing drug epidemic in Newcastle, his parents gave the *Evening Chronicle* permission to print a picture of his corpse. The paper launched its 'War On Drugs' campaign, which Cheryl backed wholeheartedly, pledging, 'I'm in total support of John Courtney's family in raising awareness about the devastating effects of heroin addiction.'

In 2007, Cheryl, sickened by the media's positive portrayal of notorious rock junkie Pete Doherty, would use her friend's untimely death as a warning to her fans in an interview with Piers Morgan in *GQ*. 'His mother crumbled to a five-and-a-half stone wreck by the end, because he'd even steal Christmas presents from his family to feed his habit. And then to see pictures of Doherty glamorizing it, and with Kate Moss on his arm, too. It makes me sick. Heroin is devil's dust, it ruins lives and families, and everything it touches. I've seen what drugs do to people.'

She went on to tell Piers that it broke her heart to see her friends and family go through the horror of drugs and admitted, 'It put me off for life . . . Smackheads tell so many lies. You convince yourself they're going to change, you're blinded by love. Yet the man you love is spaced out in bed all day. It's so destructive for everyone around them. I don't feel sorry for addicts, they know what they're doing. Kids may have been offered a spliff twenty years ago, now it's smack that can kill them. Leopards don't change their spots.'

Speaking to *OK!* magazine, tough-talking Cheryl offered no sympathy to Pete Doherty. 'I couldn't give a shit about him and I don't care if I never see a picture of him again . . . He's had umpteen chances to get off it in rehab but it's clear that he doesn't want to . . . It's not living, it's existing . . . It's devastating and I hope kids realize that it's not the right life to lead.'

While her honesty shocked the media, John's mum was only too proud that Cheryl had spoken out and was backing her campaign to stamp out drugs.

'To hear her speak out about drugs like that was fantastic for us and I just wish more celebrities would do it because they're role models to people,' she told the *Chronicle*. 'This just shows how down to earth she is and how she'll never forget her roots. She's done well for herself and lives down in London but made sure she got in touch when he died. As she said, heroin is the devil's dust, and that's why we decided we had to do something. We said from the start that if we could save one life by starting the campaign it'd be worth it.'

Chapter 5
WANNABE POPSTAR

As Cheryl reached her late teens, romance was beginning to play a larger part in her life, but, ever ambitious, she remained focused on becoming a star. At sixteen she decided the best way she could concentrate on kicking off her career was to leave school and forget about further education; a decision that her father Garry wasn't all that happy about. 'I told her that I thought she should go to college so she had something to fall back on,' he remembered on the E4 documentary series *Girls Aloud: Off the Record* in 2006. 'But she said I would be eating humble pie when she got on *Top of the Pops* and I have to admit I'm eating a big slice of humble pie now.'

Cheryl was determined to prove to her father that she'd made the right decision. She knew that she had what it took to make something of herself; she just needed a lucky break. Fortunately, things seemed to go well for her as she was swiftly signed to a management company at Metroland in Newcastle (attached to the Metro Centre), the largest indoor funfair complex in Europe. While it might not sound like the most prestigious of venues, the Metroland was the perfect place for breaking in new talent, with up to 20 million visitors a year. The complex was also the place where local kids could get to see their favourite music acts on stage, as well as offering up-and-coming local talent the chance to perform in front of an audience. Having been signed up by the company's management team, Cheryl was now on the way to fulfilling her dream of singing.

Over the next few months, the plucky songstress gigged at the complex on a regular basis, running through a couple of new songs a night. Singing to as many as a hundred people at a time, she took her job very seriously and planned her stage routines meticulously. In the daytime, she'd spend hours rehearsing at the Newcastle Dance Centre so that her moves were tight and slick. The centre's principal, Michael Conway, who had first taught Cheryl when she was ten, knew that she had what it took to take her talent to the next level. And as the man who had previously taught such superstars as Ant & Dec and Donna Air, he clearly knew talent when he saw it. 'Cheryl always wanted to be a star,' he told the *Mirror*. 'She had charisma and lots of talent but she also worked very hard to learn her routines.'

Michelle Heaton, who found fame in the original *Popstars* TV show and was one-fifth of the band Liberty X, remembers meeting Cheryl several times on the Metroland circuit. 'I first met Cheryl when I was about eighteen and in a band called Inside Vision,' Michelle recalls. 'We'd both been signed up by the same management company at Metroland so we used to cross paths whenever we were gigging at the same time. She was very cute, and of course gorgeous, and you could see the boys in the crowd going wild for her whenever she performed. She sang all the latest R&B and hip-hop tunes that were popular at the time. She loved R&B and she'd wear dungarees and trainers and look very much the fly girl.

'Needless to say, with her gorgeous face and big smile, she went down a storm at shows and when she supported boy band Ultimate Kaos, she managed to outshine them and appeared so confident and professional that it looked like she'd been on the circuit for years. She definitely had something special, so I was not that surprised when she did so well on *Popstars.*'

Another famous face who remembers Cheryl from her early days was *Big Brother* star Michelle Bass, who, having grown up in Newcastle, would often go to the Metro Centre, where she saw Cheryl sing on a number of occasions.

'I never knew her on a personal level, but I used to see her performing at the Metro Centre all the time,' Michelle recalled. 'She used to wear tracksuits and have her hair in a pony tail with a big fringe. Some people said she looked like a chav, or a charver as they call them up that way, but I think she looked good. The song she used to sing quite a lot was a track called "I'm Gonna Get You" and her performance would normally consist of her doing the splits. In great big sweatpants!'

After a period of gigging locally, Cheryl took the plunge and moved briefly to London where she was signed up by management company Brilliant, which was run by Nicki Chapman, a judge on the original *Popstars* who would later become a leading figure at Simon Fuller's 19 Management. Here, she spent her time traipsing around the city auditioning or playing showcases. It was tough for Cheryl, as this time she was in the big smoke all by herself, while Joan remained at home constantly worrying about her – even though Cheryl was all grown up now and had more confidence than she had when she was training at the Royal Ballet.

And Joan's concern wasn't completely unfounded. It was hard for Cheryl to make her mark in London. Although with Brilliant's backing she managed to land a few gigs as a session singer and very nearly a record deal, solo success still seemed out of reach.

So, reluctantly, Cheryl had to return home to Newcastle. She worked in bars to make ends meet, which left her feeling forlorn. Was she ever going to achieve her goal of fame? Or had she experienced the best of her opportunities already, destined to remain in Newcastle serving customers drinks and flashing them a flirty smile?

It was while she was working at Tyneside's floating nightclub Tuxedo Princess that Cheryl met a customer called Richard Sweeney. 'He was totally smitten by her,' a friend of Richard's remembered in the *Mirror*. 'The minute they started dating, they were inseparable, and Richard thought perhaps he had finally found his Miss Right.' But little did he know that waiting just around the corner was something that would not only end his relationship with Cheryl but would also change Cheryl's life forever.

When Cheryl heard the news in early 2002 that a new series of *Popstars* was to hit TV screens, she knew her time had come. Two years previously she had sat at home with her mother Joan, feeling frustrated that she was being forced to watch Noel Sullivan, Myleene Klass, Kym Marsh, Danny Foster and Suzanne Shaw form the reality band Hear'Say. It also hit her hard that

Michelle Heaton, whom she knew from her Metroland days, and the other wannabes who failed to get into Hear'Say went on to form their own band, Liberty X, which would go on to dominate the charts with their cooler R&B sounds. Fame and success seemed so close to Cheryl and yet so very far.

As she read the front-page stories about both bands, Cheryl was devastated that she hadn't been part of the process, that she hadn't had the chance to shine and show the world what she could offer. Every time she heard Hear'Say's 'Pure And Simple' on the radio or read about how the record had broken first-day sales, her heart ached, wishing that it were her up there performing and being photographed. It didn't even bother her when Hear'Say's star took a sudden tumble, and the records stopped selling by the bucketload: she still felt that she wanted what they had.

But then her dreams appeared to be answered. A year after Gareth Gates and Will Young had been turned into chart-topping household names on *Pop Idol* came the news that TV producers were seeking wannabes to take part in a new show called *Popstars: The Rivals*. Inspired by the chart battle between Hear'Say and Liberty X, producers decided that, instead of creating just one shiny pop band, they would form a boyband *and* a girlband, and then pitch them against each other in a race for the Christmas number one. And this time round, it would be the record-buying public who would ultimately choose who made it into the band's final line-up. Before that could happen, a set of judges would have to whittle down the thousands of hopefuls to just twenty – ten boys and ten girls. And producers had lined up some of the top names in the industry to choose who made it through.

One of the illustrious judges was the legendary pop producer Pete Waterman, who, with Mike Stock and Matt Aitken, had hijacked the charts in the late eighties with hundreds of Hi-NRG pop gems such as 'Never Gonna Give You Up', 'I Should Be So Lucky' and 'You Spin Me Round (Like A Record)'. Waterman's star waned somewhat in the nineties, so when Simon Cowell asked him to join the judging panel of TV talent show *Pop Idol* in 2001 it gave him a fresh focus for his career. It was thanks to his success on that show that the *Popstars: The Rivals* judging role followed.

The second judge was Geri Halliwell, one-fifth of the mighty girl group the Spice Girls. Although some commentators suggested she might not have had the best of voices, she was considered the driving force behind the colourful girl quintet that became not just a chart-topping global sensation but a money-making brand. Geri's role as a judge was inspiring to Cheryl. Like the Geordie wannabe, Geri had been determined from an early age to become a star and spent years auditioning for all sorts of media work. She tried out as a TV presenter on *The Big Breakfast*; she auditioned for films such as *Tank Girl*; posed topless; and had even flown out to Turkey to appear as a hostess on game show *Let's Make a Deal*. But it was when she answered an audition in *The Stage* seeking girls to join a band that her life was totally transformed, and the Spice Girls legend 'Ginger Spice' was born.

Band manager Louis Walsh completed the line-up of judges. Although he was relatively unknown in the UK at this point, he was the man behind such massive chart stars as Boyzone, Ronan Keating, Samantha Mumba and Westlife. He'd also previously appeared as a judge on the Irish version of *Popstars* in which he formed a boy-girl combo called Six. It was also on this series of *Popstars* that Louis Walsh first stumbled across a young Nadine Coyle, who would later become one of Girls Aloud. With her stunning looks and powerful vocals, she had actually made the final line-up of the band. However, when it was uncovered that she was actually sixteen years old and not the required eighteen, she was swiftly replaced by Sarah Keating.

So the new series of *Popstars: The Rivals* promised plenty. Well-known judges, star talent and a public vote. Cheryl knew that this was what she had been waiting for. And she was delighted when her application for the show was accepted and she was asked to attend a callback in Glasgow. For the first time in a while, Cheryl felt that her dreams might just come true after all.

Chapter 6
BOOT CAMP

Cheryl Tweedy was nervous, more nervous than she had been for a long time. As she waited to meet the judges, dressed in a floral top and jeans, she quaked in anticipation. This is what she'd been dreaming about all these years and now for the first time pop stardom was almost in her grasp. Only three people stood in her way – Pete, Louis and Geri.

Cheryl's fear of rejection was overwhelming. At times, she felt that she might be physically sick from nerves, while at other times, she simply felt like turning on her heel and heading back home where she wouldn't be crushed by bad news. But she knew that if she did that, she'd be turning her back on her destiny and everything she had worked so hard for. Pulling herself together, Cheryl knew that she had nothing to lose by staying. However, doubt gripped her once again when she was finally seated outside the audition room, with just a door separating her from the very people who would determine whether or not she would become a star.

Eventually her name was called and Cheryl stepped into the room with her heart thumping loudly in her chest. As she descended the stairs, she drew breath when she saw Louis, Pete and Geri looking back at her with big smiles on their faces. Even though she wasn't really the kind of girl to be star struck, she couldn't help but feel a little giddy that she was actually sharing oxygen with a world-famous Spice Girl, a legendary pop producer and the man responsible for Westlife.

When she took her spot before them and introduced herself, the old feisty Cheryl returned and she sounded confident as she announced that she was planning to sing S Club 7's classic chart-topper 'Have You Ever?' She began to sing and the nerves she had experienced earlier faded away as she lost herself in the gorgeous melody of the Cathy Dennis-penned hit. When she'd reached the end of the first chorus, the judges stopped her, their faces full of delight. She immediately knew that she had impressed them, but she hoped that it was enough to put her through to the next round.

Louis was first to speak and it was clear by his enthusiasm that he was particularly taken with her performance, especially when he declared that he wanted her in his band straight away. However, he didn't make it easy for Cheryl, grilling her on just how much she wanted the job. 'Do you really want to be a pop singer?' he asked. 'You do know it's a tough life – it's early mornings, late nights and lots of bull****.'

Cheryl hastily assured him that being a popstar was all she'd ever wanted and that she was prepared for anything that came her way if it meant that she would be successful. Meanwhile, Pete Waterman had sensed that Cheryl had been a little awkward during the audition and told her that she couldn't be nervous if she wanted to succeed. However, he admitted afterwards that he had been mesmerized by what he described as 'the most beautiful eyes and skin' he'd ever seen in his life and commented, 'You'd have to be dead if you didn't think she was stunning.' Geri, who had said little during Cheryl's audition, said she was gobsmacked by how 'stunning' and 'gorgeous' the Geordie was.

When Pete told Cheryl that she was going through to the next round of auditions in London, her heart exploded in her chest. She had done it. She had got past the first stage and was on her way to becoming a popstar! But even though she was delighted with the news, when she stepped back into the corridor to be greeted by *Popstars* presenter Davina McCall, she did so calmly, still unable to take in the news that life could soon be very different for her. Also at the Glasgow auditions was one Nadine Coyle, the gorgeous pop wannabe who had been unceremoniously kicked out of Irish *Popstars* band Six, when it was discovered she was too young. Now she was back – and seventeen – which meant she was old enough for *Popstars: The Rivals*. She impressed the judges with a rendition of Sting's 'Fields Of Gold', after which a grinning Louis boasted: 'This is my girl. I won't let her escape. She's a star!'

Meanwhile, at the Manchester auditions, Sarah Harding impressed the judges with Steps' 'Last Thing On My Mind'; Kimberley Walsh gave it all she had as she sang 'Where Do Broken Hearts Go?'; while Nicola Roberts received mixed reactions from the judging panel when she sang Shakira's hit 'Underneath Your Clothes'. Louis said she was 'nice but not brilliant' but Geri pushed for her to go through to the next stage in London.

Cheryl, excited and buzzing with confidence, moved down south once again, this time to join the hundred-plus lucky hopefuls who would be put through their paces during the workshop part of the show. Here, she knew the hard work was about to begin. It was here that the judges would be able to test the wannabes' vocal skills and dance ability in controlled conditions. So far the gaggle of eager auditionees had proved that they could carry a tune without accompaniment. But could they sing just as well with a pianist? And, more importantly for any all-singing, all-dancing boy- and girlband, did they have rhythm and could they remember dance steps?

It was around this time that Cheryl decided to call time on her relationship with Richard Sweeney. She knew that these auditions were a once-in-a-lifetime experience and if she were to give this opportunity her all she had to focus on it one hundred per cent. And she knew balancing a singing career with a long-distance romance would prove to be difficult. So, Cheryl decided it was best that they split. According to a friend of Richard's, her shock decision devastated him, as he'd hoped one day to marry her.

'When Cheryl auditioned for *Popstars* and finally knew her big break was about to happen, she broke it off with him,' the same friend told the *Mirror* years later, on the eve of Cheryl's marriage to Ashley Cole. 'He was heartbroken but there was nothing he could do. That was nearly four years ago but he still carries a torch for her and won't hear a bad word said against her. She hurt him very badly but he doesn't blame her. He would have loved her to become Mrs Sweeney instead of Mrs Cole.'

Richard himself has admirably kept his feelings about the split to himself all these years and gallantly turned down many big offers to do a kiss-and-tell. He broke his silence only once, to shower Cheryl with praise.

'Cheryl is a lovely girl,' he told the *Daily Mirror*. 'She has always wanted to be where she is now. She has been through some rough times and now she is living her dream. I wish her all the best.'

Back on the show, on the first day of workshops, the judges refreshed their memories by getting the auditionees to sing *a cappella* once again. Some shone just as brightly as they had before, while others failed to repeat their earlier performances. When all hundred or so youngsters had been seen, the judges called the anxious hopefuls to the stage again, girls on one side, boys on the other. A glum-looking Pete Waterman wasn't happy.

'We are disappointed in the auditions we've seen today,' he said gravely, causing Cheryl and the others some anxiety. 'Certainly those who stay past tonight need to up their game five hundred per cent.'

The judges then began to read out the names and numbers of contestants they wanted to form a third group at the centre of the stage. As the thirty or so names were called, the wannabes looked at each other as they wondered what the roll call of names could mean. Cheryl grew anxious. Her name hadn't been called and this new group comprised of boys and girls she remembered having performed well during the auditions. Was her dream about to end?

When the judges finished calling out names, Cheryl's heart sank. She knew it: she hadn't been called and it was time for her to go home. What had she done so wrong? She thought she'd delivered a great performance. However, she couldn't mope for long, because Pete suddenly announced that the new group that had been formed were actually the ones who would *not* be returning tomorrow. Cheryl sprang triumphantly into the air. She'd done it, she'd passed the first hurdle; but she knew that she couldn't relax. As Pete had warned, the remainder of the wannabes had to pull out all the stops if they were to make it through to the final thirty.

The next day, the remaining hopefuls were put through their paces in the dance studio. Under the watchful gaze of the choreographer, the boys and girls were tested on how good and fluid they were on the dancefloor. At the end of that, a second handful of unfortunates was culled.

Thankfully, Cheryl, with her years of dance expertise, sailed through easily. However, over the next day, her confidence was given a knock when Geri decided that she and fellow hopeful Emma Beard were too similar-looking to be in the same band. The girls were asked to show off their dance skills to see which one could bring more to the future band. Emma commented afterwards that she thought she stood no chance against Cheryl, who she knew had been taught dance from an early age. Both performed so strongly, however, that for the time being the pair were both allowed to carry on through the competition.

For the next two days, the competitors underwent further intense vocal and dance training, then eventually Pete, Louis and Geri sat down and decided which of the lucky few would make the all-important final thirty. The week had proven to be a tough one for Cheryl, emotionally and physically. Even though she had excelled at dance and shown herself to be a capable singer, she couldn't help but think that perhaps the judges would see something else, something more in one of the other contenders.

The nervous fifty were called in to see the judges one at a time. Each had to enter one of two rooms, where either Pete Waterman or Louis Walsh would be waiting for them, and make an agonizingly long walk to take a seat in front of a judge, in what was referred to as the 'green mile'. Then Pete or Louis would pass judgement, either crushing or giving life to the dreams of the eager youngsters.

When Cheryl strode across the room, tears were already streaming across her face. 'It's been so emotional,' she explained to Louis as she sat down in front of him. After a little beating about the bush, Louis broke the news she'd been dying to hear – she was through to the final fifteen girls. Cheryl was ecstatic and no longer cared that tears were rolling down her cheeks, because now they were tears of joy. But still she didn't let herself lose grip of reality. She knew the journey wasn't quite over yet: the fifteen girls had to be further whittled down to ten, a decision that the judges would make between themselves, based on the auditions so far.

With the week of workshop auditions finally over, it was time for everyone to say their goodbyes to each other, not yet knowing which goodbyes were for good. And what better way to do so than by throwing an end-of-week party. Of course, this wasn't their first night of partying. All through the week, a handful of hardcore contestants had taken to commandeering someone's room at the Thistle Hotel near Hyde Park in London and cracking open a few beers.

'The parties were wild,' contestant and eventual member of One True Voice Jamie Shaw recalls. 'There weren't any drugs involved but plenty of booze. And everyone was sexually frustrated so there was lots of snogging going on behind closed doors.' The young pop wannabes partied hard, sometimes drinking straight through to the morning. However, as a result of their wild late-night revelry, many would wake up the next morning with sore heads and croaky voices; the guilty were always detected by the judges who could spot a hangover a mile off.

But this final night was a massive blow-out. Without a care in the world, the rowdy gang, relieved that they no longer had to prove themselves to the judges, hijacked the hotel bar and in a few hours practically drank its contents. Cheryl was just so pleased that she could finally relax and not have to worry about learning dance moves or hitting the right notes until she found out whether she had made it through to the next stage.

As the evening progressed and the booze continued to flow, Cheryl caught the eye of fellow contestant Jacob Thompson. A handsome carpet-fitter from Leicester, Jacob was a popular competitor who, with his boyband looks and confident vocals, many felt had what it took to make it all the way to the final stages of the competition. No one was surprised then when the judges decided he would be one of the final fifteen. However, his journey getting to this stage almost came to an abrupt halt when he arrived at the first auditions in Manchester. When he swaggered in to meet the judges, all three were impressed by his looks, with Geri in particular captivated by his handsome boyband features and his astonishing green eyes. However, one thing bugged her – his George Michael-style beard. 'Lose the beard and come back and see us,' she advised encouragingly.

Desperate to impress, the gorgeous Jacob went away and

did just that, returning shortly afterwards clean-shaven and slick, and looking even more irresistible than before. And it was these dashing looks that caught Cheryl's eye on the first day of auditions. Better still, when they spoke, they discovered that they had a lot in common and conversation came reassuringly easily. Frustratingly their schedule over the week had put paid to their getting to know each other as well as they'd hoped, so the pair certainly made sure that this last night in London was not a wasted opportunity. After talking for a while, it was clear that they both wanted to be more than just friends.

But while Cheryl was lost in Jacob's attentions, little did she know that her joy was causing heartache for another of her fellow *Popstars* wannabes. Sixteen-year-old Jamie Shaw, who would eventually land a place in the final *Popstars* boyband One True Voice, had fallen head over heels in love with the Geordie beauty.

'When I saw Cheryl for the first time at boot camp I was immediately smitten,' he remembers. 'Out of all the girls, she really stood out in the crowd with her cute dimples and quirky attitude. I thought she was just beautiful. At the start she seemed quite shy but as she progressed through the competition she came out of her shell. But I think that was because the judges were blown away with her looks and her performances and gave her a lot of positive feedback and compliments. I think she felt her confidence grow.'

Jamie's crush became very difficult for him to deal with as the week progressed. He knew that he didn't stand a chance with her, especially now knowing that Cheryl and Jacob were an item. 'He was so manly and handsome, the competition was a little tough for me,' he confessed. 'But he was a really nice guy and Cheryl seemed absolutely besotted by him. I have to admit I was so jealous. But I was just happy to be her friend. She was so kind and so caring. Sometimes we'd sit in her room and talk about all sorts; about our families, our lives. She told me personal things about her family that I will never tell because I still respect the fact that she confided in me and she listened to me.'

The next day, after the party, and oblivious to the fact that she had left a broken-hearted young man behind her, Cheryl headed back home where she would have to endure the long wait to find out if she would be chosen for the final ten girls. After a week of such emotional highs and lows, life back home was something of an anti-climax. Much as she loved to be back with her family, she found it incredibly frustrating. She knew now more than ever that she wanted to make it into the band. Her week in London had been so amazing, and she had experienced a taste of what life might be like for her if she made the final cut. She had sung her heart out, danced her feet off and tried to soak up as much advice as she could from her mentors.

Cheryl had also found love – or what she thought might be the early stages of love. And while she waited for the day when the judges would put the wannabes out of their misery, at least she had Jacob. Luckily they were able to keep in touch with one other by phone and arranged to meet again whatever the outcome of the competition.

Then, a few days after the auditions, the moment she and all the other hopefuls had been waiting for arrived – when the three judges jetted around the country to inform them all which of the fifteen boys and fifteen girls would make the final twenty.

When Geri arrived at her door in Newcastle, Cheryl was a bag of nerves. What news had the former Spice Girl brought? Had Cheryl impressed the judges enough with her abilities? Or had Geri decided to pick her doppelgänger Emma Beard for the final ten, thus making her own place in the band redundant? Cheryl led the global superstar into her family's sitting room to discover her fate.

As they sat facing each other on the couch while the camera crew set up, Cheryl tried desperately to read any clues in Geri's face. But Geri gave nothing away: even when the cameras started rolling she looked stern and emotionless. 'Do you want the good news or the bad news?' she teased. 'The comments are that we thought you held back. We could tell that you did not give your all. As a performer you're beautiful, you absolutely blew us away. You're absolutely stunning looking and there are a lot of people that loved you.'

Cheryl wasn't sure where Geri was going with this. She'd said some negative things and some positive things. Did this mean she was in or out? She had seen in the previous series of *Popstars* that at this stage of the game the judges played with contestants, convincing them that the journey was over only then to reveal they had made it through. Could this be what Geri was doing?

Geri continued: 'Do you feel positive about your week?' Cheryl replied, 'I'd like to, but not at the minute.' Her heart sank. This wasn't going as well as she'd hoped. Was she about to stumble at this last hurdle and miss out on this chance of a lifetime? Only Geri had the answer. 'Okay,' began Geri, 'that was the bad news . . . because you're in.' The words that tripped off Geri's tongue echoed in Cheryl's ears. 'You're in! You're in!'

Cheryl couldn't believe it. She had done it: she had got through to the final ten. She squealed and threw her arms around Geri and squeezed her as tightly as she could. But then her joy and elation turned to mock anger and the feisty girl jokingly told Geri off for her wicked ruse. 'You shouldn't do that,' she joshed. 'That was really horrible. You shouldn't be allowed to do things like that to people.'

Sadly, in another part of the country Louis was in Leicester telling Cheryl's beloved Jacob that his journey was now over, explaining that his voice wasn't quite ready to go any further. Gorgeous Jacob was devastated, not only because he had crashed out of the competition at such a late stage, but perhaps also because deep down he realized that this blossoming romance wouldn't last if Cheryl continued in the competition.

Meanwhile in Wales, Jamie Shaw was delighted to discover that he had made it into the final ten boys. This meant he was in line to become a TV star and potentially one-fifth of a brand new boyband that would win the hearts of thousands of girls – and perhaps even the heart of Cheryl.

_____ Chapter 7

THE FINAL COUNTDOWN

Cheryl heaved her bags through the door of the plush £6 million mansion in Oxshott, Surrey, where the girls were to reside for the course of the competition. It was like nothing she had ever seen before. Beautifully furnished, it had all the mod cons you'd see in a superstar's house: hi-tech sound systems, plasma TVs and a kitchen full of handy gadgets.

The rooms were huge, the garden expansive, and at the back of the mansion there was a tennis court. If the girls fancied a relaxing break, they had the choice of slipping into the jacuzzi, the sauna or the steam room. But the most exciting feature of the house was the massive indoor swimming pool, which the girls immediately fell in love with. The closest most of them had come to living in a house with a pool was when their parents had filled an inflatable paddling pool with water when they were kids. This was a whole new world to them – most of them had grown up in a working-class environment – but this was a world, they realized, that they could quite possibly be living in if they made it through to the band.

All the girls knew that they now needed to outshine each other during the live shows if they were to make the band. Having reached this stage, Cheryl felt very confident in her ability and believed she had a good chance. She knew her success depended not only on her own performance, however, but also on those of the other girls, whom she considered just as strong and confident as herself.

And indeed they were a formidable collection of singers. There was Sarah Harding, the self-confessed 'loon' from Stockport; Lynsey Brown from Salford, who had already become close chums with Sarah; doll-like blonde Aimee Kearsley, who at just sixteen was shy and gentle; Chloe Staines, a redhead from Chelmsford; Nadine Coyle, Louis's old Irish *Popstars* winner; London-born Javine Hylton, who the judges thought was the UK's answer to Whitney Houston; smiley Kimberley Walsh, who'd been hastily brought in to replace a pregnant entrant called Hazel Kanaswarn (who had turned out to be too old to take part in the show); and savvy Nicola Ward from Croydon.

The final girl was Emma Beard, from Northampton, the sweet young singer who Geri had said looked so like Cheryl that she thought only one of them would be able to make it through to the band. Although she remembered from the auditions that Emma was one of the nicest of the girls, Cheryl couldn't help but worry that her position was vulnerable and that she and Emma would be in direct competition.

It was soon clear that it wasn't just Cheryl who was affected by the stress of the competition: she and eight of the girls were rocked by the news that Nicola Ward had decided to walk out on the show just days before the live shows kicked off. While host Davina McCall would announce on the girls' first live show that Nicola had quit for personal reasons – she had previously admitted that she had been missing her fiancé – Nicola later revealed that she wasn't happy with the contract the girls had been asked to sign.

'They are trying to make us sign our life away,' she was reported as saying in the *Mirror*. 'The contract is outrageous. If we win, we have to sign up to an agreement which means they own us. They can use our faces on mugs, band duvets and God knows what. And we'll only get £1,500 a week for touring while they're raking it in. They'll be making profits from ticket sales, T-shirts, TV interviews and paying us a pittance.'

She also said the recent demise of Hear'Say was warning enough of the pitfalls a band created through a reality show could face. Instead, she said she was keen to concentrate on her own solo career, a career that would, sadly for one so ambitious and talented, never materialize.

Even though Cheryl understood Nicola's reasons for quitting, she was willing to take a gamble. If the band became big, then one day perhaps she and the girls could take control of their destiny and renegotiate their contract as the Spice Girls had done before them. For now, Cheryl was quite happy to 'sign away her life', as Nicola had put it, if it meant that her dreams would finally come true.

While the house was sad to see Nicola go, her sudden departure meant there was a gap that needed to be filled. And the lucky girl to be given a second shot at stardom was flame-haired Nicola Roberts from Runcorn. Although she had made the final fifteen, Louis had initially described her during the audition stages as 'nice, but not great'. However, the judges reckoned that she had a certain something that set her apart from most of the wannabes – and that she could be the Ginger Spice of the band.

Instead of receiving the news via one of the judges, producers of the show had a much more devious way of informing her about her good news. She was invited to appear on the ITV2 extra show, hosted by Dane Bowers, to 'talk about her experience on the series'. Midway through the conversation on live TV, however, the former Another Level hunk broke the news that she was now in the running to land a place in the band. Nicola couldn't believe the news and was in a 'total state of shock' that, after her initial disappointment, she had been given a second chance!

So, with days to go before the live shows kicked off, a jubilant Nicola moved into the house and was immediately befriended by Cheryl. The pair of them were very similar, sharing the same sense of humour and a very ballsy forthright nature. In the house, they shared a bedroom with Aimee, and all three would chat about all sorts of things, such as boys and what they planned to do if they didn't end up in the band. It was this close friendship that would give them the strength over the subsequent weeks to survive the tough live stages of the show.

Although nerves were beginning to affect the girls, Cheryl was able to distract herself from the upcoming live shows by losing herself in Jacob, who despite his disappointment was making the extra effort to travel all the way down from Leicester to see her. Behind the producers' backs, Cheryl would slip out of the mansion at night and go to meet her beau at a secret location where they could enjoy an evening together.

Even though he knew that Cheryl only had eyes for Jacob,

Jamie Shaw, who lived nearby with the rest of the male finalists, still couldn't stop thinking about her. He'd even confessed to her that he liked her more than as a friend. Cheryl's reaction was sweet and she told him she felt flattered but said that at sixteen he was too young for a woman of nineteen like her. He may have received the brush-off from Cheryl, but it still didn't stop him from harbouring desires for her. 'I knew she was out of my league,' he remembers. 'But I thought it was worth a try. She was just the most beautiful girl I had ever met.'

Eventually, word got out to the papers that Cheryl and Jacob were seeing each other. At first there was talk that the relationship might have been a way for the couple to give their profile an extra boost on the show. 'Their relationship was plastered all over the papers and the teen magazines,' Jamie recalled. 'Some thought it was all just a publicity stunt, but she always used to tell me she did feel something for him and I believed her.'

Sadly, the blossoming romance would soon be nipped in the bud. It was rumoured that the show's PRs suggested to Cheryl that perhaps it was better for her to focus on the show and not get distracted by boys. The result was that Cheryl and Jacob parted company, just days before the live shows were about to begin. It was a hard decision, but in the end Cheryl felt it was the right thing to do.

'It's a shame, but we don't have time to see each other any more,' she said a few weeks after the split in the *Sun*. 'We didn't get a chance to get to know each other properly.' But whether it was her decision or not, Cheryl didn't have time to mourn the loss of her relationship: she had a TV show, and the opportunity of a place in a girlband to worry about. Luckily for Cheryl, she and the girls had a week's reprieve because the boys –

Jamie Shaw, Mikey Green, Daniel Pearce, Anton Gordon, Matt Johnson, Chris Park, Peter Smith, Keith Semple, Nikk Mager and Andrew Kinlochan – were first up to battle each other for a place in the band.

After the boys had performed an opening number as a group, they each took turns to sing their own carefully chosen song. When all ten of them had sung, host Davina opened the phone lines and asked the public to make a life-changing decision – to choose their favourite male star.

A couple of hours later, on the results show, Davina announced that Chris and Andrew had received the lowest number of votes. It came as no surprise to either of them, since they had both been criticized by the judges after their perform-ances in the earlier show; but the prospect of being booted off at this stage was almost too much to bear.

As Davina stalled over revealing which of the two boys would be saying goodbye to their housemates and to the competition, Cheryl sat in the audience looking on, aware that she too could find herself in danger of being kicked off. However, that was still a week away. For now, her heart went out to the two boys whom she had befriended over the last few weeks. She didn't want either of them to go, but she knew that it was all part of the process, and hoped that neither boy would be too devastated by the result. In the end, it was Andrew who pulled in the fewest number of votes and bid farewell to the competition and his new friends.

A week later, it was the girls' turn to showcase their talents to the nation. Although nerves had been nagging her all day, Cheryl was confident that her rendition of The Foundations' classic 'Now That I've Found You' would ensure she wouldn't end up wallowing in the final two. During the rehearsals in the afternoon, she had given a strong performance. But when it got round to the proper live show, she felt more nervous than she had so far.

When Davina announced her name, Cheryl strode out onto the stage and took her spot. As she waited for a VT clip about her week to be played out, she looked anxiously into the audience, searching out her mum for support. And there was her family beaming back at her, their faces filled with pride. Cheryl felt strong again. With her family's backing she knew she could pretty much do anything.

The clip ended and the introduction to Cheryl's number sprang into life. As she waited to sing her first line, her heart beat fast and her stomach felt empty; but when it came to hitting that first note, the exhilaration she felt was amazing. The next minute and a half whooshed by in a blur, and when she sang her final note she couldn't believe she had made it through the song so quickly. Even better, no sooner had the music stopped than the audience had burst into rapturous and almost deafening applause. If the volume of their clapping and cheering was anything to go by – with a considerable contribution from the Tweedy camp – then Cheryl reckoned her position on the show would be safe for another week at least.

The judges' comments were good and as she returned to her seat at the edge of the stage, she felt confident. Her future now lay in the hands of the great British public. Had she done enough to win over the Saturday night TV audience? Well, there was nothing else she could do but wait and watch the other girls try their hardest as they belted out their numbers.

In the results show screened later in the evening, Davina

started to announce which of the girls were safe from eviction. Cheryl bowed her head and closed her eyes, hoping she'd make it through. And when she heard her own name pass Davina's lips, she felt jubilant, as if she'd won the whole competition. But the exhilaration of surviving another week was dampened when it emerged that Kimberley, whom Cheryl had grown fond of, and Lynsey, who was Sarah Harding's close friend and roommate, were the two with the lowest number of votes.

Then, finally, Davina announced that the journey was over for Lynsey. Lynsey was devastated by the decision but seemingly not half as much as Sarah, who dissolved into tears. Although Cheryl was relieved to be safe, losing one of their number brought home to the girls just how vulnerable they were and how none of them had control over their ultimate destiny on the show. Their journey back to the house was a sombre one, knowing that over the next few weeks, four more girls would have to experience this cruel cull.

The following week it was the boys' turn again, but this particular show took a soap opera-like turn when Peter stepped forward and dramatically announced that he had decided to quit the show because he had lied about his age and was actually too old to be taking part in the competition. Although the melodramatic move was later viewed by cynics as premeditated and stage-managed, the gasp from the audience at the time sounded genuine and even Davina looked surprised by the news.

Peter explained that seeing Andrew get kicked off the show a fortnight before had made him realize that he couldn't carry on depriving the other hopefuls of landing a place in the band. The boys all burst into tears at their friend's revelation and decision, and the girls in the audience couldn't contain their emotions, while the judges and the host seemed taken aback.

So after another night of drama passed, Peter headed home and the competition resumed as normal. But unfortunately for Cheryl, week two proved much more difficult than the first. Going in to the live show, Cheryl was feeling confident, and when the introduction started to Shania Twain's 'Still The One', she wasn't half as nervous as in her first performance. As she launched in to the mid-tempo number, Cheryl seemed a lot more in control than before. With positive comments from the judges, Cheryl left the stage with reason to expect that she would be safe for another week.

However, in the results show later in the evening, Cheryl was upset to discover that her performance hadn't impressed the TV audience as much as she had hoped, and she was devastated to find herself in the bottom four. Luckily for her, Davina revealed that Kimberley and Chloe were the ones who had received the lowest votes and that Chloe was the hopeful whose dreams were now sadly over.

The experience of coming in the bottom four was devastating to Cheryl and she never wanted to be in that situation again. She knew if she wanted to survive in the competition she had to make sure that her next performance was a show-stealer that would make her stand out from the crowd.

In spite of her fears, Cheryl managed not to dwell on her unhappiness for too long. In fact, being kicked off the show was the last thing on her mind when she got to meet boyband Blue behind the scenes at *CD:UK*. Although she wasn't their biggest fan, she had danced to their songs many times in the clubs back home. And what girl wouldn't be excited to meet gorgeous pop pin-ups? Here she was, nineteen-year-old Cheryl Tweedy from Heaton, backstage at one of the biggest music shows in the country, breathing in the same air as Blue – who seemed just as excited to meet her as she was them. Duncan James and Simon Webbe both bathed Cheryl with kisses when they were introduced, and admitted that they thought she was very beautiful.

However, Duncan put Cheryl's nose out of joint by revealing that he was rooting for Javine – though he hastily added that he liked Cheryl and Aimee, too. Meanwhile, the band's wild man, Lee Ryan, boisterously bounded up to her and announced at the top of his voice that he thought Cheryl was 'fit'. In fact, so stunned was he by her natural beauty that, as he was leaving, he could be heard chanting, 'She's fit! She's well fit,' all the way along the corridor until he'd left the building.

Cheryl was left dumbstruck – never in a million years did she think she'd have *bona fide* hunks like Blue not only stopping to talk to her but being impressed by her looks. 'For the first time in my life I'm speechless,' she admitted. However, in spite of their praise, she didn't seem too over-awed by the meeting when she was asked about her experience on *Popstars: The Rivals Extra*.

'I think it's every teenage girl's dream to meet Blue,' she told presenter Hayley Evetts. 'But to be honest, I look at them as normal people. I was excited, don't get me wrong, I've listened to their songs on the radio, but they look exactly the same as they do on the telly.' And when she was asked if she had a favourite member, Lee Ryan was probably gutted to hear that she didn't.

But meeting Blue paled in comparison to the night that she and the girls got the chance to kick up their heels and rub shoulders with the rich and famous at the launch party for Westlife's greatest hits album, *Unbreakable*. The night was spectacular and not like anything the girls had ever experienced before, tucking into cocktails and champagne. Their evening had started out in style when they'd been picked up by a blacked-out limousine from their house and were then transported like royalty to the centre of London where they partied the night away with stars such as Ronan Keating and It-girl Tara Palmer-Tomkinson, as well as the Westlife boys. The evening was a blast as the girls got to experience what life could be like for them if they made it into the band. Sarah was in fun mode all evening, while Nicola Roberts was thrilled just to be breathing in the same air as Westlife, as she had been a lifelong fan of the band.

Later in the week, the girls sampled their first taste of tabloid exaggeration when the papers reported that Sarah Harding and Kian Egan were now dating and that young Aimee had snogged the band's Mark Feehily in a dark corner of the party. Bearing in mind hunky Mark would later come out as gay, the stories now sound like tabloid spin. Nevertheless, as the girls sat around their kitchen table flicking through the papers, they were amused and excited that they were considered newsworthy enough to be written about.

After the thrill and elation of partying with the A-list, Cheryl returned to earth with a bump when, in the next girls' round, she found herself languishing in the bottom two, even though she had pulled off a well-received performance of Sinead O'Connor's hit 'Nothing Compares 2U'. Louis had declared that her rendition of the song was 'absolutely great', and that he'd have no qualms about putting her in the band, while Geri congratulated her on picking a good song. But those positive comments weren't enough to keep her out of trouble, and she felt winded when Davina announced that she and her best mate in the house, Aimee, were the two with the lowest votes. To Cheryl, this was a lose-lose situation. If she was eliminated, then her journey was over and she'd have to go back to real life. But if she did carry on in the competition, it meant that she would be losing her pal Aimee, with whom she had bonded so well and shared so much.

In the end, it was Cheryl who would survive another week, which meant sixteen-year-old Aimee had to say goodbye to the world she had become accustomed to. Aimee's exit hit Cheryl hard. She even said that she wished she'd have been kicked off instead of Aimee. 'I would have preferred to have gone so that she didn't have to go through it. She was only young,' Cheryl said on *Popstars: The Rivals Extra*. 'I was only nineteen, but I'd taken knocks, I was stronger.'

That night, back at the house, Cheryl commiserated with Aimee: their journey together had been a fun one and neither wanted to say goodbye. Aimee packed up her stuff and left the house for the final time. But determined Cheryl couldn't afford to let Aimee's departure get her down for long. There was just one more week to go before the final line-up of the band was decided. And nothing was going to get in Cheryl's way. She was going to make it into the band, no matter what.

Chapter 8
WHICH GIRLS ARE ALLOWED?

The moment had finally arrived. After weeks of auditions and singing on live TV in front of millions of viewers, Cheryl and her five remaining housemates were about to discover which of them would wake up the next morning as fully fledged popstars. Having performed their final songs, there was nothing more they could do: their future lay in the hands of the great British public. Sitting on stage on the orange *Popstars* sofa, waiting for Davina to announce the final band members, Cheryl was trying to predict what might happen in the next few minutes.

In many people's minds, Nadine and Javine were shoo-ins, no question about it. Nadine had received universal glowing praise practically every week and had been described as a new Mariah Carey and Celine Dion rolled into one. Even Cheryl had to admit that her voice was faultless and probably the best in the competition. On the final show she had sung 'I Wanna Dance With Somebody' which she attacked with gusto. And her hard work had paid off; the judges loved her. 'Great job –

there was a bit of a wiggle – let go and do your own thing,' Geri gushed; while Louis beamed, 'This band will be the start of a long career for Nadine Coyle.' Pete proved just as impressed and described her performance as 'fabulous'.

Meanwhile, Javine was also proving popular. Described by many as the UK's answer to Whitney Houston, she was the contestant with the powerhouse vocals and that dash of urban cool that some thought would give the final band an all-important edge. Her final performance was a rousing rendition of Chaka Khan's 'I'm Every Woman'. When she finished the song, the audience went wild and the other girls had looked at each other and agreed that Javine was in the band for sure. The judges seemed to agree. 'So impressive,' was Geri's input. Louis then confidently declared, 'She's got soul – great performer – has to make the band.' And Pete concurred, stating, 'She's in the band – no question.'

So where did that leave the rest of the girls? Kimberley's version of Diana Ross's 'Chain Reaction' had gone down a storm, with Louis declaring it a 'fantastic performance' and Geri likening her to J.Lo, while Nicola's lively take on The Pointer Sisters' 'I'm So Excited' received great comments from the panel, including 'You walked it' from Pete and 'She'll make the band' from Louis. Sarah's enthusiastic performance of 'Holding Out For A Hero' also got her the thumbs-up from the gang, with Geri summing up her appeal by describing her as a sexy girls' girl.

And what had they made of Cheryl's tender take on Richard Marx's 'Right Here Waiting'? Well, Louis simply said, 'Vote for her!', while Geri described her as 'gorgeous, photogenic and emotional'. Cheryl picked up on the fact that Geri had not referred to her vocal performance, and Pete too avoided mention of her singing prowess, and instead praised Cheryl for being one of the nicest kids and said he 'felt for her'. He felt for her? Did that mean he didn't hold out much hope for her in the show?

What made it worse for Cheryl was that if her performance on the night wasn't enough for her to win, she'd also be disappointing her family and friends who had spent the week campaigning on her behalf. Among them was her pal John Mulroy, who had gone out of his way to produce a forty-foot-long banner that bore the words 'Vote For Cheryl, *Popstars: The Rivals*'. After having a word with Newcastle City Council he was given permission to hang his work from the Tyne Bridge so that motorists driving along it knew what they had to do that following Saturday. 'It's great Geordies support their own,' he said. 'We all want Cheryl to do us proud. And we're sure she will. But it's down to the viewers to make a difference.' And it wasn't just close friends who were drumming up support for the local celebrity. So too was the *Evening Chronicle*, which produced its own 'We're Backing Cheryl' banner. One thing was for sure, Cheryl wasn't alone in her fight for fame.

But the time for fighting and self-reflection was over. Davina stood, ready to announce the final line-up: behind her on stage were five stools that the band members would take, just as Jamie Shaw, Daniel Pearce, Anton Gordon, Keith Semple and Matt Johnson had done one week previously, forming One True Voice. Just a matter of minutes stood between Cheryl and one of those seats or a tearful journey home.

The tension in the studio became unbearable. The giddy audience were chanting the names of their favourites. From where she was sitting, a nervous Cheryl could make out lots of shouts for Nadine and Javine, but she wasn't sure if she could hear her name as much. Looking into the crowd she could see her mum and family waving and shouting, doing their part to get behind her.

Before Davina reeled off the names of the five lucky girls she asked the judges for their final comments. Louis was first to speak: 'I'm looking for a good pop band like the Spice Girls – there's no others out there.' Pete reassured the girls that whatever happened they were 'all winners' and all had careers. Geri merely advised the girls to enjoy their future journey and relish it as 'it's a precious time'.

In her seat next to Javine, Cheryl knew that in the next few minutes her life could be changed for ever. As Davina readied herself to announce the first name, Cheryl squeezed Javine's hand. 'And the first person in the band is . . .' Cheryl swallowed hard as she waited for that all-important name. It had to be Nadine or Javine, for sure, she told herself. Who else could it be? But Davina had a surprise in store as the first name called was '. . . Cheryl.'

Shooting to her feet, the triumphant Cheryl punched the air, hugged Javine and locked eyes with her jubilant mum bouncing up and down in the audience. She couldn't believe it. The dream had come true: she had made it into the band. The public had decided that they wanted Cheryl Ann Tweedy in the country's newest girlband. She couldn't believe what was happening. This kind of thing only happened to other people, not wannabes from Heaton.

As she tottered across the stage to be congratulated by Davina, tears welled in her eyes. What was going to happen to her next? How would her life change now? How would she cope moving away from home and living with a bunch of strangers?

But these questions had to wait; Cheryl was desperate to find out which of the girls would be joining her on her amazing journey. And she didn't have to wait long. The next name Davina called was Nicola, who got to her feet looking rather shell-shocked, followed by Nadine, who embraced Davina tearfully. This just left Kimberley, Javine and Sarah on the edge of their seats. As Javine had proved so popular with the judges over the weeks, would Kimberley or Sarah be the one to wave goodbye to her dream? The next name called was Kimberley, and it was looking more and more likely that Sarah was the wannabe set to go.

Davina called Sarah and Javine out to join her on stage. Before she put them out of their misery, Davina asked the judges what they thought about the way things had turned out. Geri sat on the fence: 'I love both girls – let the public pick who they want,' adding, 'These two gave their strongest and most confident performance – both can have a solo career.' Pete summed up the dramatic evening perfectly: 'It's a hell of a way to finish the series.'

So now the moment had arrived. Was it going to be Sarah or Javine joining Cheryl and the girls in the band? Adding to the tension, Davina announced that everyone would have to wait until after the commercial break to find out who the final member of the girlband was. Over the next four or five minutes, the successful four held each other close, happy that they had been chosen but also gutted that they were about to lose a good friend. Cheryl was very close to both Javine and Sarah. With Javine she'd spent hours talking through the nights over the past few weeks; with Sarah Cheryl had had loads of fun, because Sarah was wild, witty and always larking about. Whichever one went home, she'd be upset for either girl not to make the band.

Commercial break over, there was no more pussy-footing around and Davina revealed that the final person to make it into the band was '. . . Sarah.' The gasp of shock from the studio audience could be heard by viewers at home, and Sarah instantly dissolved into tears, while a dazed Javine merely stared blankly ahead of her. The revelation had come as a shock to everyone, most of all the soulful Londoner who had been told time and time again she had a guaranteed place in the band. Even Davina was shocked by the results and told her, 'I don't understand this – you are too good for the band. You are a star in your own right.'

While Sarah went to join her new bandmates, with tears still streaming down her cheeks, members of Javine's family ran up on stage to comfort their girl. However, even as their friend was coming to terms with losing out on this great opportunity, the chosen girls had to start looking to the future as Davina revealed that the name of the new band would be Girls Aloud, and that one of the songs making up the Christmas double A-side would be a cover of the East 17 classic 'Stay Another Day', which happened to be the first single Kimberley had ever bought!

Later, after the girls had celebrated backstage with their families and friends, Cheryl and the band were whisked to a nearby hotel. The following morning they had to be briefed, meet the press and appear at their first photo-call, which would involve them standing in front of a big poster bearing the ingenius slogan 'Bye Boys Buy Girls'. As she crawled into bed exhausted, Cheryl could sleep soundly knowing that, after all these years of working so hard, she was now one-fifth of a pop band that had been signed to a major record label. And with Polydor behind them, she knew success was pretty much guaranteed.

For the time being, however, Cheryl and her Girls Aloud bandmates had another battle to prepare for – the fight to gain the Christmas number one spot. The press said the boys had the battle all sewn up because they had legions of girl fans, and traditionally boybands do better than girls. But the girls were willing to work hard and it just so happened that their first single would turn out to be a surprise secret weapon that would eventually blow the boys out of the water.

Chapter 9
BEAT THE BOYS

It was 16 December 2002 – the day that One True Voice and Girls Aloud were set to go head to head in the charts. The boys' debut song was a Pete Waterman-produced cover of a Bee Gees song called 'Sacred Trust', which was to be backed with a more soulful-sounding original song called 'After The Love Has Gone', which had been co-penned by band member Daniel Pearce.

So confident was Pete that the boys would triumph with their double A-side that he pledged, 'If this song gets to number two, I will commit suicide. I have got to beat Louis Walsh.' Meanwhile, it emerged that Girls Aloud's lead single would be a drum 'n' bass-inspired dance track called 'Sound Of The Underground', that Samantha Mumba had turned down, with 'Stay Another Day' as the B-side. The girls were stunned when they were first played the track, as Nadine recalled. 'The first time I heard it, I was like, what the **** is this? It had a drum 'n' bass beat, these mad wee surfie guitar bits. It wasn't like a pop record. We had to be taught how to sing like that.

Not to leave anything spare.' Kimberley agreed that the sound was closer to the underground than to the pop charts but was pleased that it didn't have that cheesy Steps vibe to it. However, she did have concerns that perhaps the song might be a bit too cool for the pop-buying public. 'I think we all thought it was ****ing crazy!'

When the records were released to radio, the public were finally able to make their choice. The boys' tune was universally lambasted as lacklustre and sounding closer to Pete Waterman's eighties output than anything in the charts at the time, while the girls' efforts stunned the nation with its catchy melody and credible, stylish and distinctive sound courtesy of production team Xenomania. While it was clear that the girls had the better of the two songs, they wondered if the record-buyers were indeed ready for such an unusual pop tune. Would young female fans vote with their hormones and buy the boys' record with the cute guys on the cover? The girls thought so and decided just to enjoy the ride and take pleasure in the fact that their song was considered cooler.

With just days to go before the singles' proper release, the girls discovered just how much hard work went in to being a popstar when they were told they had to shoot a video for the single in a freezing cold, disused London warehouse at 5 a.m. sharp. When they arrived, Cheryl and her fellow bandmates were surprised to see how large the production crew was. As they wandered inside, tired but with eyes as wide as saucers, it felt as if they had just walked onto a Hollywood film set. Crew members were busy erecting a metal cage covered in light bulbs inside the warehouse, while wardrobe assistants were busy setting out costumes for the twenty-two-hour shoot.

Meanwhile, director Phil Griffin strolled around trying to find the best angles for shots while runners asked record company reps if they fancied any refreshments.

The girls, who were so not used to this way of life, took it all in, open-mouthed, before they were taken to one side and told what was required of them during the day. They were told that they would be filmed as a group singing and dancing along to a backing track in the bulb-lit cage. Then each of the girls would be shot separately for the cut-aways. The girls were then packed off to hair and make-up to be transformed into popstars.

The shoot itself was hard and tiring, but once their initial awkwardness at being in front of the camera had passed, the girls really got into the swing of things. Although she was nervous at the prospect of filming a real music video, Cheryl enjoyed everything about the day, aside from the early start and 3 a.m. finish. And she knew for sure that the long day had been worth it when she saw the finished results: the video was stunning, especially when compared to the boys' video which had them walking numbly through London's Docklands and sitting on an escalator that – rather tellingly – was going nowhere.

The week the singles hit the shelves, the battle between the two bands intensified. Both groups did the rounds of TV shows, but it was the girls with their stunning looks who landed the more high-profile interviews, including a seven-page feature in *OK!* magazine. 'The boys were dead in the water,' one journalist who would work with the girls over the years at a leading teen mag said. 'The styling was atrocious, the song a dreadful eighties throwback and just a lazy misjudged disaster. The thing is, the boys weren't to blame. Pete Waterman was the one who chose the song and gave it such an out-of-date sound ... Of course, it doesn't help that the girls were a lot more polished. Their styling was sassy and superior, the song extraordinary and their marketing campaign clever and memorable. The boys just didn't stand a chance!'

When it was revealed that midweek sales figures had the girls a little way ahead of the boys, the gloves really came off and the competition got personal. The boys, who had thought success would come easy to them, resorted to name calling, branding the girls a bunch of talentless singers.

'Girls Aloud can't sing,' Anton sniped to the *Sun*. 'So they are using their bodies. Suddenly the clothes have fallen off. They are doing everything they can to get to number one but they are making themselves look stupid.' Bandmate Daniel Pearce, also talking to the *Sun*, didn't hold back either and made his opinions very clear about what he thought of their performance that he'd seen at London clubnight G-A-Y, at the Astoria. 'They sounded so flat, they just can't sing. They can't harmonize. They tried to rescue it by getting Bryan McFadden on stage. We sing live every time. For us it's all about singing well and harmonizing. The proof will be when we tour. We will show the girls up for what they really are.'

Cheryl responded to the newspaper: 'The fans at G-A-Y were chanting "number one" to the girls and the boys weren't too happy. If they can't even sell themselves to gay men, well, it says it all, really.' The boys' mentor Pete Waterman then waded in by saying he thought the girls 'had the style and the look, but not great voices', to which Louis hit back saying that One True Voice were little more than a Westlife tribute act.

Not to be outdone, Pete then accused the girls of not actually singing on the record and told Neil Fox on his Capital breakfast radio show, 'It's a smashing pop record but unfortunately they are not on it. I've had that record since September. The version I've got is no different. It's just got four other singers on it. Just listen to the choruses – they are session singers.' First Louis threatened to take legal action if Waterman continued to spout such rubbish, then Cheryl let loose at the producer in the *Sun*: 'How did he think he was going to get away with that when people heard us sing on TV for ten weeks?'

Hurt by the personal comments made by One True Voice, she added: 'They've called us tarts and said we can't sing or dance. It's taken it beyond a joke but we're not going to sink that low. I don't know why they have taken it to this extent. They're insulting all the people who voted for us to be in the band so they're not doing themselves any favours.'

And the battle didn't just stay between the bands. The *Sun* then seemed to support Pete Waterman by stating that 'Sound Of The Underground' had actually previously been recorded by another girlband called Orchid and that the original band could still be heard on the record. The record label responded, pointing out that they had never hidden the fact that the girls could be heard singing backing vocals – and their names, Eve Bicker, Giselle Somerville and Louise Griffiths, were credited. Girls Aloud themselves added: 'Everyone uses backing vocals; Mariah Carey and Whitney Houston use them and they just make the song sound better. We're not denying it and we never did.'

The bitterness between the two bands became so ferocious that they couldn't actually bring themselves to say anything nice to each other when they came face to face on TV shows or at functions. All this saddened Jamie Shaw of One True Voice, who blames the feud on over-zealous PR: 'As soon as the rivalry started there was a dramatic change in the girls' attitudes but I know for a fact that their management and PR offices had a lot to do with it. It was from that point that we started to lose contact with each other. Which was very sad for me as I still fancied Cheryl.'

On 22 December, the results were through. The two bands returned to the *Popstars: The Rivals* studios to discover where on the charts their songs had entered. The midweek results were expected to be repeated, with the girls beating the boys, and Cheryl and the rest of the band were confident. Standing on stage looking a lot slicker and more styled than even a week before, the girls relished the fact they were to be told that they were number one at Christmas and that they would beat their rivals on live TV. But it wasn't yet confirmed, so Davina crossed to DJ Neil Fox, who was presenting the *Network Chart Show* and asked him to put the country out of its misery.

As expected, the girls had triumphed, having shifted 213,000 copies compared to the boys' 147,000. The girls exploded with joy, as they were showered in ticker tape, while the boys had to half-heartedly comfort each other. But the girls had little sympathy for their cocky rivals. 'The boys had been bigged up so much and then they didn't actually get it,' Nicola was reported as saying in the *Observer*.

So there it was: the girls had won and the boys had lost. And not only had they scooped the fifty-first Christmas number one, but the group were also the first band to score a festive chart-topper with their debut hit, and the first girlband to debut at number one. Who needed Christmas presents when the girls could boast fabulous facts like that?

Before Cheryl could head home for some well-deserved festive time off, she had one last issue to address – Jamie Shaw's continued infatuation with her. Even though the two bands had fallen out during the ferocious chart battle in the run up to the Christmas number one announcement, Jamie still had a crush on gorgeous Cheryl.

The night before the final Christmas show, Jamie, no longer able to keep the extent of his true feelings to himself, sent Cheryl a text telling her that he wanted to go out with her. He felt that if he didn't tell Cheryl about the way he felt there and then, he would never know what she might have said. But he would have to wait until the next day to find out what she felt.

'She came up to me at the show and told me that it wasn't going to work out,' Jamie recalled. 'It made me feel shit, to be honest, as my feelings for her were electric. I did cry a little, knowing I didn't have a chance in hell with her. She said to me that I wasn't her type on the outside but that I was on the inside. I felt bad but I didn't feel awkward afterwards. We both cherished the friendship that we had for the time it lasted.'

Although the pair pledged to remain friends, Jamie and Cheryl lost touch soon after that Christmas. 'We texted each other for a couple of years, but we just weren't able to see each other much,' he explained.

And so with that episode sorted out, Cheryl was able to say goodbye to her new bandmates for a short while so she could head home to spend Christmas with her family. But Cheryl's yuletide joy was about to come to a tragic end . . .

Chapter 10
HEARTACHE AND HEADLINES

When Cheryl arrived back in Heaton, she received a hero's welcome. Well-wishers flocked to her mum's house as if it were Graceland, all keen to let Cheryl know that they had helped her land a place in the band. The local newspaper, the *Evening Chronicle*, which had been so supportive to her over the years, was there to welcome back their triumphant daughter.

While Cheryl was extremely grateful for the attention and excited by her newfound fame, she wanted more than anything to spend some quiet time with her family. Having worked so hard down in London and spent so much time away from home over the past few months, Cheryl wanted just to be Cheryl Tweedy from Heaton again.

Once the euphoria surrounding her return had died down, Cheryl was able to enjoy her three-day break at home, catching up with her brothers and sister and on the local gossip. But as soon as she'd lost herself in the magic of Christmas, she was brought back down to earth with a bump when she received a call from her record company rep passing on the devastating news that the band's tour manager, John McMahon, who had driven them around the country for promotional appearances and interviews for the past few months, had been killed in a terrible car accident on Christmas Day. The forty-three-year-old, who had previously worked with the likes of Belinda Carlisle, Mis-Teeq, Craig David, Boyzone and Westlife, had been thrown through a side window of his Chrysler people carrier when it careered off the road and ploughed into a hedge and hit a telegraph pole. He had been pronounced dead on the scene near Cresswell in Northumberland.

The girls, who in the short time they had known him had looked up to John as a rock in the craziness of their new lives, were distraught by the terrible news. A heartbroken Kimberley said in a statement to the press: 'John has been with us every hour of the day since we were picked to be in the band. We feel devastated because John was a constant support to us everywhere we went. He was the one who would round us up while we were promoting the single. We really liked John. He was a father figure to us.' Cheryl added: 'We were supposed to be celebrating Christmas but we are very upset and shocked. Our thoughts are with his family.'

Cheryl and the girls started their new year by scrapping all their promotional plans to pay their last respects to the man they had grown to love, attending John's funeral at St Austin's church in Stafford. Dressed in black, the girls let the tears flow freely as friends and family spoke emotionally of their loss during the forty-five-minute service. After Louis Walsh's girlband Bellefire had performed an emotional song, John's coffin was carried out to the strains of Tina Turner's 'Simply

The Best'. The girls, so moved by the loss of their friend, would later pay tribute to him in the sleevenotes of their first album.

Sadly for Cheryl, trouble seemed to follow her around during the month of January 2003. Just days after John's funeral, her future in the band hung in the balance after she got into a brawl with a toilet attendant during a night out at the Drink club in Guildford. The evening had started off pleasantly enough when the band had gone for a quiet dinner after a gruelling twelve-hour stint at a local recording studio. Cheryl and Nicola, up for a night on the tiles, decided to join some other pals at Bar Zuca, where they spent much of the evening drinking. After enjoying several drinks there, the tipsy group moved next door to the Drink nightclub for a bop on the dancefloor.

And they weren't disappointed. The place was in full swing, with music pumping, revellers dancing and drinks flowing freely. After their stressful few weeks and their very recent loss, Cheryl and Nicola were determined to relax and have a good time. And for the most part all seemed to be going well. When they weren't on the dancefloor or quaffing champagne in the VIP lounge, they spoke happily to onlookers who recognized them from *Popstars: The Rivals*. In fact, they appeared to enjoy the attention they were attracting, no doubt because they'd only been proper popstars a matter of weeks and the novelty of signing autographs and having total strangers approach them was still fun.

But when Cheryl and Nicola ducked to the loo, problems ensued. According to thirty-nine-year-old toilet attendant Sophie Amogbokpa, trouble started when Cheryl started grabbing lollipops and a bottle of perfume from her display table. When Sophie asked Cheryl what she was doing, she allegedly replied, 'My father owns this place. I can do what I like,' and made for the door. The attendant grabbed an angry Cheryl by the arm and pulled her back and made her drop the goods into the sink.

At this point, Nicola apparently dashed off into the club to find a security guard to calm things down. Meanwhile, the attendant alleged that, as she began to replace the items Cheryl had taken, the singer began shouting racist comments at her and then, just as Nicola returned with the security guard, Cheryl allegedly launched herself at the attendant and punched her in the face.

Phil White, the club's head of security, also told the *Mirror* a couple of days after the incident that he had to pick Cheryl up and carry her to the other side of the toilet to calm her down, but she kept flailing and shouting out racist comments at Sophie. Phil said he then escorted her to the VIP lounge where she was ordered to apologize to Ms Amogbokpa. But Cheryl apparently continued to rant about the attendant and kept on slapping her fist into her hand threateningly. Police were called and Cheryl was taken to Guildford Police Station, where she spent the night in a cell.

The experience wasn't pleasant. 'It was scary there,' she said on *The Frank Skinner Show* in November 2003. 'It was cold, it smelt funny, like that bleach smell from school. I just sat on the bed and sobbed. And pressed the buzzer around twenty-five times. I was able to make one call and I called my mam straight away!' Meanwhile, Nicola had returned to the hotel where the girls were staying to break the news to them that Cheryl had been carted off by the police. 'We were like, "No way!"' Kimberley recalled on *The Frank Skinner Show*.

'We couldn't get our heads round it. Then we went downstairs and the police were there to take Nicola's statement.'

Back at the cell, Cheryl felt scared. She'd never been in trouble with the law before and she felt so alone. All she wanted was her mum to come and hold her in her arms. As she sat there, gradually sobering up, she began to wake up to the enormity of what had happened. Getting into a brawl – for whatever reason – was stupid in the position she was in now, and she was scared that her new record bosses would come down hard on her. She'd only been a popstar a month or so and now it looked as if she could be on the verge of losing her job already. She couldn't believe what was happening.

At eleven the next morning, Cheryl made a statement to the police claiming she'd acted in self-defence and had never referred to the toilet attendant as 'a black b****' and then headed to ITV studios to appear on *Ant & Dec's Saturday Night Takeaway*. There was talk of pulling out of Ant & Dec's show as Cheryl was sporting a juicy shiner, but thanks to the expert skills of make-up artist Christopher Ardoff, Cheryl managed to go on stage without anyone guessing she'd been involved in a scuffle.

Speaking to the *News of the World* two days after the incident, Cheryl told a very different story to the one Ms Amogbokpa had recounted. 'We saw these lollies, took one each and went to do our make-up. The attendant started shouting, "Oi, you're supposed to leave money." I said, "We'll pay when we leave." She then called me a bitch so I told her to get lost. She punched me in the face and then I hit her back and called her a "****ing b****". When I got to the police station a doctor was called to examine me because I had a swollen cheek and some scratches, but I got the all-clear.'

Cheryl also hit back at the claims that she had racially abused the toilet attendant. 'I am not a racist. Javine from *Popstars*, who is black, is one of my best friends.' She also revealed that when police had read her Ms Amogbokpa's original statement, there had been no reference to any racist slur. 'I only acted in self-defence because I was hit first. I admit I may have called her a b**** in the heat of the moment, but I never made any racist comments to her. I am distraught that people are accusing me of racism. It couldn't be further from the truth.'

Concerned mum Joan was quick to defend her daughter and to quash the suggestion that she was racist in any way. 'Cheryl is a quiet, sensitive girl who has never been in any trouble,' she told the *Sun*. 'I can't imagine she'd start the fight. She is obviously devastated at newspaper reports of what she is supposed to have said to this woman.' Joan also pointed out that Cheryl had long enjoyed the music of black artists and had dated Haydon Eshun from boyband Ultimate Kaos during her Metroland days.

'She grew up loving music made by coloured artists,' Joan said. 'Cheryl has been speaking to Javine and she has given her full support. Cheryl has had boyfriends from the ethnic community and has friends who are black. To call her racist is really out of order. All I know is she has been left very upset. She feels her name has been dragged through the mud.'

A panicked Polydor rep issued a hasty statement explaining how Cheryl deeply regretted getting into the fight and that she was shocked and absolutely distraught when what she was supposed to have said to the toilet attendant emerged. Although the record label appeared to be standing by her, rumours were rife that Louis Walsh and record chiefs were seriously considering dumping Cheryl from the band, bearing in mind the band's young fanbase.

However, Louis stepped forward to stand by his charge. 'She made a mistake and didn't handle things very well,' he acknowledged in the *Mirror*. 'But there are two sides to every story. It's very easy to point the finger and accuse the famous person of being in the wrong. She knows what she did was wrong and I have spoken to her about it but I'm not giving her the boot from the band. I have told the girls that they have to be on their best behaviour from now on because they are in the spotlight.'

One True Voice mentor Pete Waterman used the incident to lay into Girls Aloud, no doubt still smarting that Louis's girls had beaten his boys in the charts. 'It's bad behaviour, of course it is,' he said to the *Mirror*. 'There's absolutely no need for it. If you go to a nightclub and have too much to drink you're fair game and people will have a go at you. You just don't go to those places if you can't handle it.'

Luckily for Cheryl, the rest of the band pledged to support her and had no intention of making her leave them. 'We've made a pact to stand by Cheryl, regardless of what happens,' Sarah told the *Daily Star* after Cheryl appeared before magistrates in Guildford on 25 March 2003 accused of racially aggravated assault. 'We never once considered that we were going to throw Cheryl out of the band and no one else could make that decision. We're really strong in our belief that no one can take it away from us. It was really hard for Cheryl because it has gone on so long. But all you can do is be there and support her and hopefully things will go for the best.'

Kimberley would later admit on *The Frank Skinner Show* in November 2003 that the incident had rattled the band considerably but said that they had believed in Cheryl all the way. 'At the time, it scared us, we were like, "Oh my God, this is really bad," especially as we'd only just released our first single . . . At the point we found out we hadn't heard from Cheryl, but we believed Nicola's account of the story. When we saw her, we discussed what happened and we supported her from there. We always knew the race issue was going to be cleared so we never ever thought about that too much. I have to admit I was shocked when I heard that Cheryl had got into a fight, cos she had never done that before.'

Unfortunately for Cheryl, and with the trial still pending, the next few weeks would see her name continuing to hit the papers for all the wrong reasons, but this time due to her family.

A couple of weeks after Cheryl's arrest, her brother Andrew and sister Gillian found themselves in big trouble after a drunken argument turned into a street brawl. The merry siblings had enjoyed a night out on the town. Tipsy after a few drinks, they started to bicker outside the Raby pub near the pair's home in Byker. The argument became so rowdy that other revellers joined in, resulting in a brawl. When the police arrived, the fight was broken up, but more trouble ensued when the Tweedy kids got into another argument with a young couple on their way to Byker Metro station. Police were called to the scene where they found the brother and sister involved in a brawl with the couple. Gillian and Andrew were arrested and later bound over to keep the peace for twelve months and fined £100 each by Newcastle magistrates.

Cheryl couldn't believe what was happening. Just a month after experiencing the highs of winning a TV search for a star and landing a record deal, not to mention enjoying four weeks at number one with 'Sound Of The Underground', Cheryl felt as if her world was falling down around her. It seemed that the press had it in for her. Yes, she had a temper, just like the next person, but she wasn't a bully nor was she a racist. It had all been a big mistake. She knew that but how could she persuade the rest of the world reading the newspapers that she wasn't the same person they were reading about?

But things were to get worse for Cheryl. A little while later she was unceremoniously thrown out of the Baja Beach club in Gateshead after being accused of starting a water pistol fight with a group of Newcastle United footballers. Again, mum Joan, who was actually with Cheryl on the night out, was quick to defend her daughter. 'There was a bunch of Newcastle players there and they came to talk to her,' she told the *Evening Chronicle*. 'She was just standing with them. Some of them were playing with water pistols, but not Cheryl. I saw it all happen and I was horrified. The bloke who asked her to leave looked in a real strop. We were all there just to have a good time, minding our own business. I don't know what his problem was.'

No sooner had that incident passed and Cheryl's brother Andrew was in trouble again, this time for allegedly breaking into a stolen car. The press of course had a field day, using his arrest and court appearance as an example of how dysfunctional they thought Cheryl's family was, and a pack of journalists and paparazzi was waiting at the magistrates court in Newcastle when he arrived. His lawyer, Lewis Pearson, attacked the press for hijacking Andrew's case and trying to use it against his sister. 'Andrew apologizes unequivocally for his behaviour,' Pearson told a court. 'What upsets him is the fact that the press are here. His sister is a member of a pop idol band and they wish to use his conduct to shame her.'

Things were looking bad for Cheryl. Would she be able to shake off all this bad press and continue to grow and succeed in Girls Aloud? Or would all the negative stories destroy all she had achieved?

Stars in their eyes – even in her early school photos with her brother Garry, Cheryl knew how to work the camera.

Girls 3 piece suit with red fleece jacket, ski pants & black top.
Sizes: 22, 24, 26, 28, 30, 32
Normal Price £19.99
CLUB PRICE £

Her photogenic looks were put to good use when she modelled for a local superstore.

Eleven-year-old Cheryl relished her time in the spotlight as one of the tots in the Whitley Bay Pantomime Society's 1994 production of *Aladdin* (*back row, second from left*).

Ever since Cheryl was a child, her mum Joan nurtured her daughter's obvious talents. 'My mum is more like a friend than a mum,' Cheryl would later say.

Before she fell in love with singing, Cheryl dreamed of being a ballerina. However, after winning a place to attend London's prestigious Royal Ballet Summer School, she soon decided that tutus and ballet shoes were not for her.

It was clear that dancing wasn't Cheryl's only skill: she had the voice of an angel too. She discovered her talent for singing at school, and went on to land a management deal at Newcastle's Metroland leisure complex, where she sang her heart out to thousands.

Judgement night approaches for Tyneside wannabe

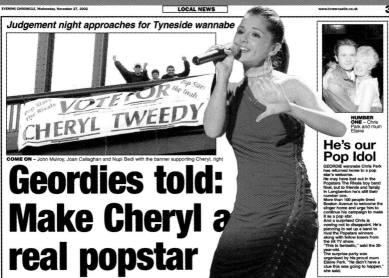

VOTE FOR CHERYL TWEEDY

COME ON – John Mulroy, Joan Callaghan and Nupi Bedi with the banner supporting Cheryl, right

NUMBER ONE – Chris Park and mum Elaine

He's our Pop Idol

GEORDIE wannabe Chris Park has returned home to a pop star's welcome.

He may have lost out in the Popstars The Rivals boy band final, but to friends and family in Longbenton he's still their number one.

More than 100 people lined Boston Avenue to welcome the singer home and urge him to continue his campaign to make it as a pop star.

And a surprised Chris is vowing not to disappoint. He's planning to set up a band to rival the Popstars winners along with fellow losers from the hit TV show.

"This is fantastic," said the 20-year-old.

The surprise party was organised by his proud mum Elaine Park. "He didn't have a clue this was going to happen," she said.

Geordies told: Make Cheryl a real popstar

By GORDON BARR
Showbusiness Reporter

FANS were flying the flag for Popstars hopeful Cheryl Tweedy as a massive banner was unfurled on the Tyne Bridge.

As the 19-year-old band final on Saturday, family and friends have been drumming up support for her back on Tyneside.

And her name was hard to miss with a 40ft-long banner asking viewers to vote for her being hung on the Geordie landmark.

It read: Vote For Cheryl Tweedy, Popstars The Rivals, and got toots of approval from passing motorists.

Newcastle City Council gave Cheryl's mum Joan Callaghan and friend John Mulroy permission to display the flag from the busy bridge for a couple of hours.

And when they took it down, it was back up again almost immediately - at the Breeze Bar/Cafe on Newcastle Quayside.

Cafe owner Nupi Bedi has been a family friend for years and was only to happy to display the banner on his premises.

They are all hoping it will encourage viewers to vote for the Geordie lass, from Heaton, as she tries to make it into the final five in the girl band on Saturday's crunch show.

Millions of viewers saw Geordie Chris Park lose out in the boy band stakes last Saturday - now North East hopes are pinned

HOORAY – Heaton youngsters are right behind Cheryl

on former Walker Comprehensive pupil Cheryl.

"It's been a real rollercoaster of a time for her," said proud mum Joan.

"She hasn't been home for three months, but I've been to every show she has been singing on, and I get to see her afterwards.

"And I am in daily contact with her. Whatever happens on Saturday, Cheryl will remain level-headed.

"She met Westlife recently and wasn't starstruck. She believes everyone is the same, whether you are a big star or whether you are begging for money on the streets.

"And I know she won't change, whatever happens. She is so down to earth."

Childcare worker John Mul-

roy, 21, has known Cheryl for years and has been drumming up support for the singer.

The five to 12-year-olds at his Kenton After School Club have been voting like mad for the teenager, and it was John's idea to put the banner on the Tyne Bridge.

He contacted Newcastle City Council, who gave permission for it to be displayed for a couple of hours.

"It's great," he said. "Geordies support their own – we all want Cheryl to do us proud.

"I'm sure she will. But it down to the viewers to make the difference."

Residents in Heaton have also been showing their support. A our picture shows, they're right behind their singing neighbour. They were only too happy to

popstars the rivals

L 786

Having seen Cheryl secure a place in the final twenty of *Popstars: The Rivals*, her home city of Newcastle rallied round to support its talented star. Her friend John Mulroy even managed to hang a banner saying 'Vote for Cheryl Tweedy' on the Tyne Bridge! (Pictured above in the *Evening Chronicle*.)

Cheryl couldn't believe her luck when she made it through to the final twenty. Nor could she believe the £6 million mansion she and the other hopefuls were to live in. Here she is seen with (*from left to right*) Javine Hylton, Aimee Kearsley, Sarah Harding, Nicola Roberts and Kimberley Walsh.

Midway through *Popstars*, Cheryl and the girls got a taste of what it would be like to be A-listers when they partied with Westlife at the boys' album launch in London.

Cheryl with *Popstars* presenter Davina McCall in the final week, as she waits to hear what the judges have to say about her version of Richard Marx's 'Right Here Waiting'.

One True Voice – the male *Popstars: The Rivals* band that would take on Girls Aloud and lose: (*from left to right*) Matt Johnson, Jamie Shaw, Anton Gordon, Keith Semple and Daniel Pearce.

'Buy Girls Bye Boys' – the slogan on their T-shirts says it all. The morning after the night before, Girls Aloud pose and flash their smiles to the press for the very first time. They are (*from left to right*) Nicola Roberts, Nadine Coyle, Sarah Harding, Cheryl Tweedy and Kimberley Walsh.

Chapter 11
SOUNDS OF GIRLS ALOUD

As the controversy surrounding Cheryl and her family continued to rumble in the press, Girls Aloud were still hard at work carrying out promotional duties for their chart-topping single, as well as planning to move to London full time. They were excited about the big move but anxious, too, as they knew it would mean that they'd have to say goodbye to their friends and family for a long period of time. But they knew if they wanted to be successful and make a go of this once-in-a-lifetime opportunity, certain sacrifices had to be made.

Their new home, after a brief spell in a block of flats in Westminster, was to be in a housing complex favoured by the rich and famous. Situated in the far north of London, it was a prime location; easily accessible for the city centre, but secluded enough for the girls to live in peace away from the prying eyes of the paparazzi and fans keen to get a glimpse of their idols. The secure gated development of four hundred luxury apartments was favoured mainly by sports stars and celebrities, and, in keeping with the flamboyant lifestyle of the famous, residents only had to step out of their doors to find facilities such as tennis courts, a health club, a swimming pool and a private bar and restaurant.

When the girls first stepped through the gates into the lavish complex, they couldn't believe that this was going to be their new home for the indefinite future. Only in their dreams had they imagined themselves living in such a plush place. However, as Cheryl took in her surroundings, she hoped and prayed that recent events wouldn't mean she'd have to say goodbye to it all too soon.

Life at the complex was fun for the girls, and when they were able to find the time, they'd make the most of the facilities on site, taking a dip in the pool or having an early morning workout at the gym. Choosing who would live with whom was easy, applying the popular maxim, 'If it ain't broke, don't fix it'. So just as they had in the *Popstars* house, Kimberley and Nadine shared one flat, Cheryl and Nicola another, while Sarah chose to live alone, which as an only child and a self-confessed 'Monica from *Friends*', was the way she liked it.

Cheryl and Nicola had become very close during the series, but since Cheryl's recent brush with the law, the pair of them had formed an even tighter bond. In fact, Cheryl admitted that her ginger bandmate made life more bearable through that tough time. 'I couldn't be in the band without Nicola,' she told *Top of the Pops* magazine in 2004. 'When we first met I thought she was shy but now I know different. Nicola is hilarious, I've never met anyone like her. Sometimes in the morning when I try to get her out of bed to go to the gym, she just grunts at us. She just growls like a dog. All she eats is McDonald's, Burger

King, Wimpy but she never puts a pound of weight on. It makes me sick – she does my head in, she's so lucky.'

However, there were some downsides to living with Nicola – not only was she a messy girl who'd leave her floor covered in clothes and fake tan smeared all over the bathroom, she had a habit of borrowing things from Cheryl and never giving them back! Cheryl revealed to the *Top of the Pops* magazine: 'She takes whatever you lend her – tweezers, lip liners, anything. You have to go into her room to look for things.'

But the girls didn't exclude their bandmates from their close friendship. They always found time for each other when they weren't working. The girls would enjoy hosting dinner parties for each other, where they'd serve up such tasty delights as a big Greek salad, tomato, avocado and mozzarella salad and chicken kievs, followed by lashings of Häagen-Dazs ice cream. While the public had been given a one-sided portrayal of Cheryl in the press, Kimberley had been captivated by the real Cheryl: a sensitive, funny Geordie who could 'talk for England'.

'She likes to laugh,' Kimberley once commented on her pal in *Smash Hits* magazine. 'Once she's telling a story she'll tell it thread to needle – from beginning to end – and you'll not be allowed to move a muscle.' She also described Cheryl as 'cute and sweet' and admitted that she always wanted to mother her. 'When I first met her I thought she looked young, sweet and innocent ... That's not entirely the case – she's not that innocent. She's a bit of a party animal; when she goes out she has a good time.'

But there weren't many opportunities to party at that point in time, as the girls were busy recording their debut album. Not that anyone expected much from the results. With 'Sound

Of The Underground' still riding high in the charts, rival stars readily stepped forward to predict a short-lived career for the group. Duncan James, who had met Cheryl backstage at *CD:UK* during the *Popstars* programme, reckoned they'd go the same way as their predecessors Hear'Say. 'Their first single will be their highest-selling song,' he declared in the *Sun*. 'It will be the peak of their career and if you start at the top the only way is down. It'll be exciting for the first six months, but after that, they'll be isolated, insecure and paranoid, not knowing who they can trust.'

Whether that warning was based on his own experiences was unclear, but the girls ignored his negative comments and believed that they could achieve whatever they wanted to and outlive the original *Popstars* band. 'It really p***es me off when people keep going on about what happened to Hear'Say,' Cheryl said in the *Observer*. 'Gareth [Gates], Will [Young] and Darius and Liberty X are all doing okay. We're doing okay. Hear'Say are the only ones that failed.'

But could the naysayers be right? An eleven-date UK tour planned for March, which would have seen One True Voice and Girls Aloud travel around the country's arenas, had been scrapped due to poor ticket sales. Was this a sign that the girls were already on the wane? Not in the slightest, Louis Walsh argued. He blamed the lack of interest on the fact that no one wanted to pay good money to see Pete Waterman's dated boyband. 'Being associated with One True Voice was not doing the girls any favours,' Louis was reported as saying on the BBC news. 'Girls Aloud are doing brilliantly and they don't need to be supported by anyone else.'

And so the girls banished that setback from their minds and

threw themselves into what they hoped would be a spectacular first album. Based on the success of the debut single, which had surprised critics with its cool, cutting-edge sound, producers Xenomania began to piece together a collection of songs that would push the boundaries of traditional girlband music.

Brian Higgins, the brains behind the outfit, and his team of songwriters are well respected in the industry, having produced many chart hits for stars such as Dannii Minogue, the Sugababes, Cher and Saint Etienne. They were determined to ensure that Girls Aloud were not going to be one-hit wonders or sneered at for releasing tinny disco hits. Brian Higgins had loftier ideas. 'What we stand for,' he said in the *Observer Music Monthly*, 'is everything about the interesting side of music but with tunes that the postman will whistle.' And that's exactly what he produced for Girls Aloud.

The album certainly wasn't like any other pop album around at the time. The second single, 'No Good Advice', sounded nothing like the previous hit but was just as ground-breaking. Gone were the drum 'n' bass beats, and in their place was a punky, attitude-filled sound. Elsewhere on the album, there was an acoustic-sounding ballad called 'Life Got Cold', which the tabloids would later suggest had been heavily inspired by a musical phrase in Oasis's 'Wonderwall', and a Hi-NRG disco track called 'Girls Allowed', which came courtesy of Westlife's Bryan McFadden. Nineties popstar Betty Boo, aka Alison Clarkson – who had penned Hear'Say's mega-selling debut single, 'Pure And Simple' – was called upon to write and produce tracks called 'Boogie Down Love', 'Love Bomb' and 'Mars Attack', while former B*witched singer Edele Lynch had a hand in co-writing 'Some Kind Of Miracle'.

By March 2003, the single 'Sound Of The Underground' had gone platinum, selling 600,000 copies, so whatever followed had a lot to live up to. But those worries were forgotten when the record label heard the finished album. They loved it and knew they were onto something big. In spite of what their critics thought, Girls Aloud would be no flash in the pan, they had that something special that previous reality stars – or most pop bands around, come to that – didn't have: sass, style and that all-important X factor.

Impatient to get a new song into the charts, Cheryl and the girls were excited about filming their second pop promo. The last shoot had been a cold and tiring day trapped in a dank warehouse, so the girls were pleased to hear that this new video would be shot in a proper studio. Sadly, the second experience didn't prove to be any easier than the first. Not only were they forced to dress up in space-age BacoFoil-style outfits, but they had to dance in heels around a bashed-up old pink convertible from 5 a.m. through to midnight. Worse still, Cheryl was in tears, complaining that her shoes were too tight. But ever the professional, she managed to put a brave face on her pain and discomfort, knowing that making the video look good was the most important thing. She wanted this track to be a hit and she knew that the promo had to look great if she wanted the band to be given regular air time on the music channels.

And when she saw the final product, she and the girls were not disappointed. Although they still hated the outfits with a passion, they were impressed by the pacey editing, dazzling special effects and the all-round sassiness of the song. Without a doubt, the track and the cinematic video would provide them with another top-five single.

Released on 12 May 2003, the song stormed into the charts at number two, shifting 42,762 units in a week. Only R. Kelly with his slinky hit 'Ignition' kept them from reaching the number one spot. But the girls weren't too upset; they were more focused on their album. And in this business, the album was the money-spinner. Released a week later, it too entered the chart at number two, behind Justin Timberlake's *Justified* and, a month later, would be certified gold, having sold over 100,000 copies. Not bad going for a girlband formed on a reality show.

What was even better was that music critics had given the album the thumbs up. And not just critics from *Smash Hits* or *Top of the Pops*, either. *The Times* said it was 'one of the best pop albums you'll hear all year', while the *Sun* also tipped several songs such as 'Some Kind Of Miracle' as chart-bound hits of the future. The mighty Girls Aloud had managed to achieve what had seemed impossible – to wow not only pop fans but also hardened music critics.

The girls were thrilled with the album's success and critical reception and decided to celebrate their achievement with a flamboyant show at G-A-Y, where they performed a six-song set, dressed in saucy schoolgirl outfits. The reaction was phenomenal: the crowds of pop-loving men screamed and whistled so loudly that they could barely hear the girls sing as they ran through their set list. The special performance also gave the band a chance to stick two fingers up at boyband Busted who had recently taken a pop at them in the teen press. Spiky-haired Matt Willis had told *Sneak* magazine that Nicola was a 'rude ginger b****' after she had 'blanked' him at a gig. In response, cheeky Nicola scrawled 'Rude Ginger B**** ...

Bother'd' on the rear of her skirt, knowing that the paparazzi would snap it and publish it the following Monday, sending a very stern message to Willis!

Although the girls had been hard at it for the early part of 2003, it didn't mean that Cheryl was lacking in romantic interest. As early as January, it was rumoured in the *Daily Star* that Newcastle and England star Kieron Dyer had been asking Cheryl for a date.

According to a friend of the midfielder who talked to the *Daily Star*, Kieron had got hold of Cheryl's number after seeing her on *Popstars* and started bombarding her with calls, asking her to go out with him. For a time she apparently shrugged off his advances, but then eventually agreed to attend a match where he persuaded her to walk around the pitch at half time. But Cheryl later claimed that romance hadn't been on the cards for the two.

'I did go to a match with Kieron and I do know him, but we didn't go out on a date,' she said in the *Sun*. 'I wouldn't mind, though – I think he's really nice. But I'm single at the moment.'

Next on the rumour mill was Ultimate Kaos star Haydon Eshun, who in 2003 was back on the celebrity scene thanks to his appearance on reality show *Reborn in the USA*. The tabloids suggested that a romance had blossomed when the pair met each other at a charity bash on Valentine's Day. According to one reveller, Cheryl had made a beeline for Haydon and acted like a giggly schoolgirl around him. She and Haydon then supposedly spent several days holed up in a suite at the K West hotel in Kensington. But what the tabloids weren't aware of at the time was that Cheryl had actually known Haydon years before when she supported him and his band at Metroland, and had enjoyed a handful of dates with him.

So had romance blossomed second time round? Haydon suggested it might, telling the press that he really liked Cheryl and teasing, 'We haven't got back together but who knows what's going to happen in the future?' However, Cheryl didn't seem as keen, dismissing the rumours out of hand, commenting to the *Daily Star*, 'I was obsessed with him when I was nine. We've become friends but I'm still single.' And she cheekily told another journalist at the *Sunday People*, 'I keep hearing Haydon talking about us going out. He really ought to move on.'

As it turned out, Cheryl would find romance a little closer to home – with Kimberley's gorgeous brother Adam. The only boy and second youngest of the four Walsh children, Adam was a loyal and protective brother with a naughty streak. When he wasn't jumping out of cupboards and surprising his sisters, he'd be busy playing tricks on them. With his dashing good looks, he was never short of female attention. Although he had met Cheryl briefly during *Popstars: The Rivals*, it was only meeting her again properly for a night out with sister Kimberley and her boyfriend Martin Pemberton that Adam's feelings were awakened. The attraction was mutual and instant and the pair of them got on straight away, spending the whole night chatting and flirting.

'We just clicked and everything's going great,' Cheryl told the *Sun* at the time. 'He's like the male version of me and we're getting along just fine! Although he's living in Yorkshire and I'm always on the road, it hasn't been too much of a nightmare to see him.' Although Kimberley was happy that her friend Cheryl had found romance with her brother, she did admit that she was a little apprehensive, worried how things might work out if they ever broke up. 'It's hard because they're the two people I really love,' she said. 'If anything goes wrong, it's going to be awful.' Luckily for all concerned, when Adam and Cheryl did eventually split a few weeks later, they did so as friends.

But this left Cheryl feeling down. She was the only one in the band without a man in her life and she wasn't happy about it. 'The others found Mr Right before Girls Aloud took off,' she said in the *Sun*. 'It's impossible for me to start a relationship. We are working so hard there's no opportunity to meet someone.'

Even though the likes of Kieron Dyer and Duncan James had gushed about how gorgeous she was, Cheryl complained that no man approached her. 'I never get chatted up. It's really frustrating. I want a bloke with hidden charms but I only get approached by the cocky idiots who swagger around like God's gift. My ideal man would be 50 Cent – I wouldn't mind breeding a whole football team with him. But I'd just be happy with a builder or a postie – as long as he was a Geordie.'

However, it would be some time before Cheryl would meet the man who would change her life for ever. In the meantime, she had more pressing things on her mind. Like the prospect of going to prison . . .

Chapter 12
THE FINAL VERDICT

As she strode into Kingston Crown Court on 9 October 2003 in a tailored white suit, Cheryl Tweedy was aware that the eyes of the country were on her. She also knew that she had a lot to lose if the case didn't go her way.

Since January, practically every story written about her made some kind of reference to that dreadful night in Guildford, and it hurt her. She had been portrayed as a fist-happy bully, the kind of girl who preferred to deal with the situation physically rather than talking it through, which couldn't be further from the truth. What had happened that night had been a one-off, and, more importantly, she had merely acted in self-defence.

But what bothered her more was the fear that people might believe that the attack was racially motivated: she could never live with that. Never in a million years would she have used racist slang, no matter how angry or drunk she was. It wasn't in her make-up, and her parents hadn't brought her up like that.

Luckily, Cheryl was able to find comfort in the fact that she had the backing of her thousands of fans. 'The mail I got was amazing,' she would reveal in the *Sun* after the trial. 'I was inundated with letters from the fans telling me how much they supported me. I got poetry, too, the letters were really touching. I cried for about a week reading all that mail. I locked myself away in the flat and read them all. They really meant a lot to me.'

In spite of the support from fans, it was still imperative for her to prove her innocence once and for all. As she entered the court room she knew that the outcome of this week could affect her life for ever. This was scarier than any audition she'd ever been to. She glanced over at the jurors, trying to gauge what kind of people they were. Would they listen to both sides of the story fairly and base their judgement on the facts? Or would they look at Cheryl and see a popstar who thought she could get away with anything? She wasn't sure, but she hoped that when she would eventually take the stand, they would listen to what she had to say without prejudice.

First to give evidence was Sophie Amogbokpa, who told the court her version of events. Cheryl kept her head bowed as she heard a different story to the one she herself remembered. Sophie claimed that Cheryl had charged at her, shouting and knocking her glasses off. 'She was very aggressive and she acted violently towards me,' she remembered. 'She said "you f***ing b****" just over and over. The other girl Nicola was trying to restrain her. She was holding her and trying to calm her down.'

Under cross-examination Ms Amogbokpa was asked why she had not used the word 'black' in the original statement she had made to police straight after the incident. She paused for a moment, and admitted that she couldn't explain why reference to racial slurs was missing. Cheryl stared at Ms Amogbokpa's face as her defence attorney, Richard Matthews, accused Sophie of being the first to use violence. 'You went on the attack because you thought Cheryl Tweedy was taking too many lollies. You punched Cheryl Tweedy.'

However, far from caving in when what Cheryl believed was the truth was put to her, Ms Amogbokpa denied that she had thrown the first punch. Cheryl was crushed. Next to take the stand was Lauren Etheridge, a university student who had been in the ladies' lavatory at the time of the alleged incident. She agreed that Cheryl was 'completely paralytic' as she argued with the toilet attendant and confirmed that although she had seen the popstar lash out at Sophie, she had not heard Cheryl use any racial abuse.

Although Cheryl didn't like to hear about her drunken behaviour on the night, it was a relief to hear a witness to the event actually come out and say that she hadn't heard her say anything racist. On the second day of the trial, Drink's security manager Phillip White was called to give evidence. He told the court that when he reached the scene he saw Cheryl 'right-hook the toilet attendant'. He also told the court that when he tried to bundle Cheryl out of the toilet, she was firing off all sorts of racist insults at the toilet attendant. 'Miss Tweedy was trying to break free from me and said, "I'm going to do you. I'm going to finish the job." She said, "You ****ing black b****. I'm going to do you."' He also alleged that when Cheryl had been taken to the VIP room to calm down she had screamed, 'Get that jigaboo up here and I'll sort her out.'

On day six of the trial, an emotional and considerably thinner-looking Cheryl Tweedy was asked to take the stand. She told the jurors that she had acted in self-defence and had actually tried to get away from the aggressive Ms Amogbokpa after she had lashed out at her. 'I was thinking how in the hell do I get out of this one. She was a big woman and was scary-looking with quite broad shoulders. I felt scared of what she was going to do. I was in a strange area in a strange club. I wasn't sure of the situation. I whacked her back. I don't remember how hard. I was feeling scared, upset and angry.'

Cheryl also admitted that while she had sworn at the toilet attendant she had never uttered any kind of racial abuse and claimed that she had never used the word 'jigaboo' or indeed ever heard of it. A tear-soaked Cheryl also told the court how her life had been affected by having to live under the dark cloud of racism for the past nine months: 'It's been sickening. Embarrassing. There's no way, no matter what state I'm in, would I refer to anybody by their colour. I did not use any racist words at any time in that club.'

When prosecutor Patricia Lees suggested she had let fame go to her head, Cheryl wasn't having any of it. 'I am extremely lucky but I have worked hard for what I have got. Things had changed for me in the last four weeks but it doesn't mean that the way I was brought up and the person I am had changed. I did not use the word "black" at that woman.' There was nothing more she could do now. Cheryl had said her piece, she had told the truth and now it was up to the twelve jurors to decide which side they would take.

When Nicola Roberts took the stand that week, Cheryl felt terrible. She felt that this was her problem and she felt bad that her friend had been dragged into giving evidence. But Nicola had told her that she wanted the truth to be heard and so had no problems about having her say. During her evidence, Nicola said that it was Ms Amogbokpa who had lashed out first, while Cheryl was rummaging around in her handbag looking for change as a tip. 'Cheryl just retaliated in self-defence, as anybody would if they had been punched in the face,' she told the court.

'She was getting the change out of the bag, the lady just walked over and smacked her in the face. It was all just chaos then. I stood there and Cheryl said "Go and get the manager", so I ran out. As I came out of the toilet I saw the security guard coming towards me and I said, "The lady in the toilet has just punched Cheryl in the face." The security guard just walked in and went towards Cheryl. The lady and Cheryl were close and everybody was just shouting and stuff like that, then I saw the lady smack Cheryl.'

When prosecutor Patricia Lees suggested that perhaps Nicola had invented the story to give Cheryl a lifeline, the redhead responded: 'I'm not going to lie for anybody. At the end of the day it's my life, my career, I'm not going to lie for anybody.'

As the trial drew to a close, a couple of character witnesses for Cheryl were called to the stand to offer the jury a truer picture of the defendant. Anoop Bedi, a businessman who had employed Cheryl in a café in Newcastle, said the twenty-year-old was a very friendly and helpful person, adding that fame had not changed her. More importantly, he said, 'She might be a lot of things, but she is never a racist'. Songwriter Ricky Hanley, who worked with Cheryl before she'd found fame with

Girls Aloud, also underlined the fact that 'There is absolutely no way she could be called a racist'.

In the closing speeches, prosecuting counsel Patricia Lees painted a venomous picture of a young popstar who had let fame go to her head. 'Even important or famous people can behave very badly indeed and they have been known to do things which are wholly inappropriate to their status, particularly if they are seen as upstanding members of the community, politicians or role models, and sometimes it is a question of having too much too young. These people are not above the law, nobody is.'

She added: 'Celebrity can be a difficult thing. She was nineteen, she had a few weeks of meteoric success and she had too much to drink. Here was this woman telling her – the girl who had been taken up to the VIP suite, given champagne, announced over the DJ system, staggering out of the cubicle – telling her she has to pay for a handful of lollipops. How do you think she took it? Who do you think was behaving well or badly? The stone-cold sober lavatory attendant who might lose her job, or the drunk Cheryl Tweedy who was frankly all over the place? The defendant has a very strong motive to lie; she has a lot of things riding on it for her. She did not even know what the reaction of her new record company would be to this. She made up the lie, adapted it from her friend, who also lied, and probably thought it would never get this far.'

In her seat, Cheryl was visibly shaken. The words were ugly and so hurtful. She looked at the jurors. Were they lapping up the prosecution's every word? Did they really think she was the monster she had been portrayed as? Stifling back the tears, she waited for Richard Matthews to give the jury a truer account of who Cheryl Tweedy was.

Mr Matthews reminded the jury that Cheryl had acted in self-defence and that she had not used any kind of racist terminology. But he also wanted them to remember that the nightclub's director, Paul Endersby, had contacted a PR agent within an hour of the row because he 'wanted assistance on how best the media could be handled'. He also pointed out how the PR agent, known as Keith, had interviewed staff from the club within hours of the incident before arranging an exclusive deal for the story with the *Sunday Mirror*.

The judge adjourned the case until the following Monday, which meant Cheryl spent a restless two days thinking through all the options that lay before her. If she were found guilty of racially aggravated violence, would she be kicked out of the band? Or worse still, what if the judge decided that she deserved a jail sentence?

There was no way she'd survive a spell in prison. That one night in the cell in Guildford back in January was hard enough – spending months behind bars didn't bear thinking about. Luckily, she told the *Sun*, she had mum Joan by her side to comfort her. In Cheryl's flat in north London, cradling Cheryl in her arms, Joan told her daughter that she wasn't to worry about anything, that whatever happened, she and the rest of her family would help Cheryl get through it. Cheryl would later tell reporter Victoria Newton from the *Sun* that if it hadn't been for Joan, she wouldn't have got through it. 'My mum moved down to be with me for a week before the case. I just wanted her there with me – I couldn't have coped without her. She was my rock. I was totally useless, I couldn't do anything for myself and I was in tears all the time. She washed and ironed all my clothes and cleaned my flat. I feel awful for putting my family through all this but they were fantastic.'

On 20 October 2003, Cheryl awoke with her heart in her mouth: the accusation of racism and the prospect of a criminal record had cut her to the quick. Arriving at the court with Joan by her side, Cheryl kept her head down as the feverish paparazzi shot picture after picture. Once inside the court, it was clear to all in attendance that Cheryl looked half the woman she was at the start of the trial. Over the past week or so, she had lost around half a stone from the stress of the case and her clothes were hanging loose on her. 'I couldn't eat a thing,' she remembered in the *Sun* newspaper shortly after the court case. 'I'd put something in my mouth but I just couldn't swallow it, it was horrible.'

When Judge Richard Howarth instructed the court to rise, Cheryl felt a little wobbly on her feet. His verdict was one that could potentially destroy her life completely if it didn't go her way. The judge described the incident as an 'unpleasant piece of drunken violence' and said Cheryl had shown 'no remorse whatsoever'. He then announced that the jury of seven men and five women had found Cheryl guilty of assault occasioning actual bodily harm, but that she had been cleared of another charge of racially aggravated assault.

As a result, she was sentenced to 120 hours' community service and was ordered to pay £500 compensation to the victim and £3,000 prosecution costs. As the words tripped off the judge's tongue, Cheryl broke down and buried her face in her hands. She had never been in trouble with the police before, yet now she had a criminal record. She was angry at herself, ashamed and feeling terrible for upsetting her devoted mum who had brought her up so well. There was relief that she would no longer be seen as a racist, but it was still a bitter pill to swallow.

As Cheryl left the courthouse with her mother by her side, she wondered what the media would make of this, but her worries were laid to rest when her label, Polydor, informed her that she had nothing to worry about – her place in the band was safe. They even issued a statement to reassure fans that Cheryl was going nowhere. 'We are pleased Cheryl has been found not guilty of the main charge against her,' it read. 'In light of this decision, Cheryl's position in Girls Aloud is unaffected.'

While her fans were universally thrilled that Cheryl had been cleared of a charge that few had believed in to begin with, some media observers took it upon themselves to use Cheryl's experience as a stick with which to beat any young stars who thought they were beyond the law.

In her *News of the World* column a week after the verdict, Ulrika Jonsson had her say – and it didn't make for easy reading. 'Cheryl Tweedy from the pop group now more commonly known as "Girls A Lout" has got her just deserts. Her behaviour when she punched a toilet attendant showed she has let drink AND fame go to her head. She is an arrogant bully who, it goes without saying, sets an abysmal example to young women. However, I predict she will go solo and have a highly successful career. There's nothing like bad publicity for selling records.'

But Cheryl wasn't going to let Ulrika get away with her damning comments and told the *Sun*, 'I was furious by what she said. I just thought, "I've never met you, you don't know

me, how would you know? How dare you say that about me!"'
She went on to add: 'She says I'm a bad role model – well, what
kind of role model does she think she is? I've got news for her
– she just needs to take a look at herself and watch out if she
ever bumps into me or the girls. I was so upset that fans might
think that of me.'

In an interview with the *Sun* straight after the trial, Cheryl
paid tribute to her bandmates who she said had really come
through for her. 'Sometimes I just wanted to be on my own
but the girls were amazing. We are best friends; I'm not sure
that people can quite understand how close we are. I didn't
ever think about quitting but I did worry what it meant for my
future in the band.'

Kimberley Walsh told the *Sun* that their pal's dreadful ordeal
had made them a much tighter unit. 'What has happened with
Cheryl has actually brought us all a lot closer. It could have been
any one of us that got involved in a situation like that, where
things go wrong, and we're so lucky that we all are genuinely
the best of friends.'

And if Cheryl had any worries that the court case would have
affected the band's popularity, they were forgotten when their
single 'Jump', taken from the *Love Actually* film soundtrack,
debuted on the chart at number two in November 2003.

Cheryl carried out her community service back home in
Newcastle so she could be near her friends and family, should
she need their support. The work was tough – the complete
opposite of the glamorous popstar life of which she had
dreamed. There were no red carpets or glam frocks here. But she
didn't complain. She felt so bad about what had happened, what
she had put her family and bandmates through, that if picking

up litter and sandpapering benches at the Blue Star football ground in Woolsington would show people how very sorry she was, then so be it. She would later say that her community service had brought her back to earth with a bump.

'I had to sand benches every day and had the company of some real rough diamonds,' she told the *Sun*. 'The Geordie blokes really gave me the shake I needed. The experience was positive. I had a spell working in a care home with multiple sclerosis sufferers as well and it was really rewarding. The idea of community service sounds really grim but it made me realize just how lucky I was to lead the life I do.' She went on to explain that during her punishment no one treated her like a popstar and she was grateful for it.

'The people I was working with every day were great and didn't treat me any differently than anybody else,' she recalled. 'There was one old guy who had MS and I had to dress him and give him cereal in the morning. He was just so sweet. I really hope we'll stay in touch.'

Cheryl ended the year the way it had begun with a hero's welcome performance at G-A-Y at the Astoria club. It may have been something of an *annus horribilis* for her, but she was grateful that the fans were still behind her.

The court case aside, 2003 had been a good year for Cheryl in many respects. The band had gone from strength to strength and enjoyed four top-ten singles and a top-five album. The girls had become pin-ups and tabloid dreams, they had been lusted after by celebs and had out-lived their rivals from *Popstars: The Rivals*, One True Voice, who had split in August 2003.

Cheryl's dreams of pop stardom had finally come true, but

she'd almost lost it all in a split second of madness. So what better way to start the new year off and forget the negative events of 2003 than by giving the paparazzi a picture to remember – by giving her best mate Nicola a big kiss on the lips!

Chapter 13
LIVING THE HIGH LIFE

That infamous Britney-Madonna-style kiss shared between two friends at G-A-Y predictably had all the papers the following Monday teasing their readers by playing up its 'lesbian' overtones. But it was just a bit of fun. And that's what Cheryl wanted 2004 to be about.

With her community service out of the way, Cheryl was looking forward to focusing on life in the band and making sure it went from strength to strength. '2004 is definitely going to be my year,' she declared. 'I want to put the past year behind me.'

And so Cheryl threw herself into her work enthusiastically, and seemed to love every minute of it, even more so than she had before. When she appeared at Newcastle's Powerhouse club in early January, she was amazed by the reaction of the crowds. Even before they had stepped out on stage, the girls could hear the chants of support from the 1,400 revellers from their dressing room. And when they actually walked onto the stage, they were nearly blown away by the deafening roar of the appreciative fans. Club manager Chris Gilroy said afterwards that he had never seen a crowd like it at the popular gay venue. Girls Aloud were as sought after as ever, and Cheryl was over the moon.

For the next few weeks, the girls appeared at various shows and were pleased that they had been added to several upcoming Radio 1-sponsored gigs. There was no sign of their popularity waning as had been the case for previous reality show bands. As they merrily went about their business, they ignored comments from Spice Girl Mel C on *CD:UK*, who branded them 'pop puppets' and suggested that they'd never be the global phenomenon the Spice Girls had been. And they didn't care a jot when LostProphets singer Ian Watkins referred to them as 'braindead bimbos'.

Girls Aloud had heard all this kind of criticism before, and over the past year they had grown a thick skin. Every time a negative comment was thrown at them, they'd remember the many glowing reviews their first album had received or the joy they'd seen on the faces of their thousands of happy fans. As long as they kept their fans happy, who cared what a former Spice Girl and the frontman of a relatively obscure rock band had to say?

Meanwhile, away from the band, rumours bubbled up again that Cheryl was dating Kieron Dyer. According to reports, she and Kieron were spotted snogging in the VIP section at trendy London club Nell's. After a few drinks there, the couple allegedly made a break for it, trying to fool the paparazzi by leaving separately but then, when the coast was clear, jumping into a taxi and heading over to Trap club. There they were ushered past the red rope into the VIP area before hitting the dancefloor where they were apparently unable to keep their hands off each other.

Somewhere in the middle of all the fun the girls had to fit work in, too. Girls Aloud's work commitments saw them travelling over to Dublin to join Westlife and Gareth Gates at a Childline concert. But while in Dublin, the girls found time to attend Samantha Mumba's twenty-first birthday where they had a ball, and were later splashed across the papers leaving the party looking a little worse for wear. Although Cheryl was never happy about seeing tabloid pictures of herself falling out of clubs, the celebrity lifestyle she was now leading was the best time of her life.

The lust for fun continued when the girls got back to London, where they hit the club scene hard and made the papers almost every other day. And their wild ways did not go unnoticed. Their Polydor bosses had apparently grown concerned that the girls were living a little *too* much and with a second album to record soon, they needed to be reined in. And so they called on Louis Walsh to take them in hand and also to point out their post-Christmas weight gain. The result? The girls were ordered to shape up under the guidance of an ex-military P.E. instructor.

'The girls . . . are quite out of shape,' a band insider told the *Sun* at the time. 'So, it was decided we would put them all on a real back-to-basics regime to get them looking great again. This is no health spa they're at. It's proper military-style instruction with no frills attached. By the time they finish up in the next three weeks they are going to be in the best condition of their lives.'

So for the next three weeks, the band had to endure 6 a.m. wake-up calls, and gobble down a breakfast of porridge, before embarking on a strenuous cross-country run. After that,

Cheryl and the gang would have to work up a sweat performing agonizing squat thrusts and push-ups for an hour before settling down to a healthy lunch of plain salad with a sliver of fish or meat and some fruit. In the afternoon, the girls were hard at it again doing workouts and a few laps of the pool. Then, after a light dinner, they were ordered to go to bed at 10 p.m.

The regime may have been tough, but the results were there for all to see when the girls emerged from their training camp looking lithe. Fit, healthy and focused again, they knuckled down to work on their next album. This time round, Brian Higgins and his Xenomania team were given full control of the album and they agreed that the girls were allowed more involvement in writing.

While a year ago they had been happy just to sing along to songs already written for them, Girls Aloud had quickly learned that writing would give them extra credibility and could also be financially rewarding. And if the tabloids were right, then the girls needed to make extra cash if they wanted to lead that celebrity lifestyle. One report suggested that they only earned £80 a day, while the rest of the money made from record sales was poured back into the label to cover costs for videos and photography. Sarah stated in the *Mirror* that she was still struggling financially, saying, 'We just seem to work, work, work. I've worked like a dog and don't have much to show for it.'

Luckily for the girls, Brian Higgins was only too happy to let them get stuck in. 'We don't let them out of the room till they've given every ounce of melodic instinct that they've got in them,' Brian told the *Observer*, 'then we pile some more in. And when you listen back to the completed track at the end, they've contributed very well.' But the girls knew that however much they contributed to a song, it was Brian and his Midas touch that created the magic.

Cheryl believed that the music Brian produced for the band could only have been written with them in mind. Speaking around the time of the release of their second album *What Will the Neighbours Say?*, Cheryl said in the *Independent*: 'It would be a shame if someone like our producer Brian Higgins went unnoticed. He can't sing a note and he definitely couldn't front "Love Machine". These songs would never have come to light if it hadn't been for us. We do our best in the studio and our best to sell the song to the audience when we're out there, but the production of the songs and how good and fresh they sound, that's all down to the brilliant hard work of Brian and all the people at Xenomania. Without them there wouldn't be any of us. They are the best at what they do!'

Kimberley added: 'Brian says, "I couldn't have this kind of success without you and the whole team of people around you." The way we look, the way we are as people – all of that inspires Brian to write. We sing bits and pieces of the songs and he builds the music around us.'

With their new streamlined physiques causing a sensation, it came as no surprise that some of the girls made it into *FHM*'s '100 Sexiest Women Of The Year' chart. And this year, Cheryl was delighted to hear that she had moved up the chart from twenty-four to twenty-two. Cheryl was flattered, especially as she was the number one Girls Aloud star on the chart, having overtaken Sarah, who was at twenty-five and Nadine, who had climbed from eighty-seven to forty-six.

At the end of April, a tabloid reported that Cheryl had been seen partying with Liverpool players Djimi Traoré and Carl Medjani at Mosquito club in Liverpool. A reveller supposedly told the paper that: 'Cheryl performed an X-rated lap dance on both players before leaving the club with bandmate Nicola and her boyfriend Carl.' However, contradicting these reports, a week later Cheryl was quoted as saying that she and the single members of the band had scrapped men off their to-do list.

'We're not even thinking about men now – we've got each other and that's enough for us,' she told the *Mirror*. 'Everyone thinks you need to be going out with a man to have a good time, but that's rubbish. We feel like the girls in *Sex and the City* – but without the sex. We're strong and independent and are doing just fine without blokes.' She added: 'When we go out, we're going out to dance and not to look for men. We're probably having the best time of our lives right now.'

By the summer, the girls were putting the finishing touches to their album. They weren't too busy to accept their invitations to the *Glamour* magazine awards, however, where they were stunned to pick up the gong for 'Band of the Year'. Cheryl knew that winning such an accolade from a prestigious magazine was a big deal. Well-respected glossy *Glamour* only features a certain calibre of celebrity within its pages. Ultimately, Girls Aloud were a pop band that had been put together on a TV show – they would normally expect to grace the pages of teen mags and tabloids. But this award gave them the credibility so many like them craved.

At the end of June, the girls returned to their favourite haunt, G-A-Y, at the Astoria nightclub, to celebrate the release of the first single from their second album, 'The Show'. Unsurprisingly, the girls' wild performance went down a storm and the new songs managed to hit the right spot with the pop-loving revellers. Before the girls dashed off for the night, club promoter Jeremy Joseph crept on stage to surprise Cheryl. In his hands, he was carrying a birthday cake in celebration of her twenty-first birthday, which was coming up in a few days' time. Cheryl, beaming from ear to ear, accepted the cake and blushed as the 2,000-plus crowd sang 'Happy Birthday' in unison. Since 2004 had begun, Cheryl's life had turned right around. And in just a few weeks' time, things were going to get even better.

Chapter 14

PSYCHIC INTERVENTION

Released a couple of days before Cheryl's birthday, Girls Aloud's single 'The Show', with its kooky video in which the girls run a fifties-style beauty salon, stormed the charts and gave them their fifth consecutive top-five hit. That was swiftly followed up by 'Love Machine', a high-octane singalong which would later be covered by Arctic Monkeys on Radio 1. The song, sounding unlike anything the girls had done before, did the business and crashed into the charts at number two, only just unable to shift the dancefloor anthem of the summer, 'Call On Me' by Eric Prydz, and its overtly raunchy video.

The new song added to Girls Aloud's credibility, and the press gave the girls the credit they deserved. The *Daily Record* went as far as to say the hot and spicy five-piece were even better than their nineties counterparts, stating: 'Once upon a time Girls Aloud positioned themselves as the new Spice Girls, but it's doubtful whether Geri and Co. would have the clout to carry off such a striking pop tune.' This number-two smash was also the track that helped the girls match the Spice Girls' record of six top-three hits in a row. Cheryl couldn't believe how well things were going.

Despite saying that men were off the agenda in the summer of 2004, Cheryl had discovered that perhaps her love life wasn't as disastrous as she'd thought – and that the man who would become the love of her life had been living a few doors away all this time.

It was a blisteringly hot day in August and Cheryl and Kimberley were cruising through the housing complex, on the way to the shops. As they drove by the tennis courts, one of the tennis players called out to the girls to pull over. It was Jermaine Pennant, an Arsenal player who knew Kimberley quite well. The girls were keen to enjoy their day off and soak up a little afternoon sun, so they joined Jermaine and his friend. Although the girls recognized Jermaine's friend as his fellow Arsenal player Ashley Cole, they waited for a formal introduction before launching into conversation.

In his autobiography, Ashley recalled that Cheryl had seen him around the complex before and had been ever so slightly put off him after he'd leaned out of a mate's window to yell, 'Hey, hot lips! Nice bum!' At the time Cheryl merely rolled her eyes and thought to herself, 'Typical footballer.' Seeing him again now, she realized just how cute he was. But, for now at least, she played it cool, as if she didn't know who he was. Not the tallest of men at five foot seven and a half, Ashley made up for his lack of height with his stunning dark eyes, great bone structure and a disarming nature that simply captivated her. But as Cheryl was living under a 'no-man' rule at that point, she didn't give pursuing him a second thought. After all, there were so many stories about footballers' bad behaviour in the press, and she didn't need to complicate her life with that.

However, unbeknownst to Cheryl, Ashley had her set in his sights. Although this was the first time he'd properly spoken to her, he knew that she was the one for him. 'Here was someone on my wavelength, I knew it there and then,' he recalled in his book, *My Defence*.

When she returned from the shops, Cheryl found Ashley tinkering with his Aston Martin. She wound down her window and asked what was up. 'A flat battery,' he replied and then the pair started to chat. As the conversation continued, Ashley surprised himself by suddenly asking her for her number. Although he had no problems attracting women, the fear of a knockback is always crippling for any man. But this time he knew he had to do it: he had to see this woman again and have a proper chance to get to know her.

Reaching for his mobile, he clicked into his address book so that he could take down her number, but Cheryl had other ideas. 'I can't,' she said. 'I'm sorry but I can't.' Ashley was devastated. What was wrong? He was a good catch. He was a decent guy. Perhaps she was seeing someone? Or perhaps she just didn't like him? Either way, it looked as if his luck was out.

In actual fact, Cheryl was equally taken with Ashley but the time wasn't right for her to launch into a relationship. However, when she drove on and got home, she found that she couldn't shake Ashley from her mind.

Ashley was now besotted with Cheryl and he would constantly poke his head out the window to see if she was around. He may have been blown out, but he knew that he still had to try. After all, in training, Arsenal manager Arsène

Wenger drummed it into the boys to 'Stay touch-tight and you'll get your man'. And so he kept his eyes peeled on the complex grounds, desperate to catch sight of his crush.

Meanwhile, Cheryl was beginning to question her 'no-man' rule. The more she saw him in the newspapers, the more she thought about him. And when she was flicking through a copy of *Zoo* in a local shop and came across a piece on Ashley, she couldn't help thinking that perhaps this guy was worth a shot after all.

The next time she saw Ashley, she made an extra effort with him, calling out, 'See yourself in the magazine? Looking good!' Ashley waved back shyly and flashed her a smile, but secretly he wondered if her comments were genuine or just her attempts to mock him.

During a brief stop-off in Newcastle a while later, Cheryl visited a psychic for a private reading. As a believer in the paranormal, Cheryl occasionally visited psychics. And on this occasion, she was stunned by what she heard. Midway through the reading, the psychic told her that there was a footballer in her circle whom she had just seen in a magazine, and to whom she would be married by the age of twenty-four. This was all too much of a coincidence. Ashley fitted the description, but with all her dilly-dallying, had she missed out on happiness with the man she was destined to marry?

Without wasting another minute, Cheryl got Kimberley to text Jermaine Pennant her number so that he could pass it on to Ashley, which he dutifully did. Like a typical man, Ashley didn't act straight away and toyed with the number for a full week before he mustered up enough courage to send a text at around 1 a.m., thinking that she'd be tucked up in bed and asleep, saying 'Fancy meeting up?' He was astonished to get a text straight back from Cheryl that said, 'I'm still awake. So how are you?' It turned out that Cheryl and the girls had just finished a gig in Scotland and Cheryl was finding it hard to come down with all the adrenalin coursing through her veins.

Ashley was thrilled. This was looking good. It seemed that after a slow start, he had managed to get his woman. Arsène Wenger had been right about staying touch-tight. And so the couple started seeing each other and Cheryl was pleased that they appeared to click straight away.

'I wasn't looking for a long-term relationship,' she said of their early days together, 'but pretty soon after I met him, I knew I had never felt like that before.' And, better still, when Cheryl eventually introduced Ashley to her parents, they welcomed him into the fold with open arms, despite the fact that he played for a London club.

'My mum really approves of him,' Cheryl said to the *Sun*. 'Going out with an Arsenal player may not have been the best thing to have done but he plays for England too, so he gets away with my dad . . . just!'

For their first proper date, Cheryl and Ashley went to see his favourite soul singer, John Legend, in concert. However, it wasn't the most romantic of dates – as Kimberley and her hunk boyfriend Justin Scott came along for the ride, too. When they got back to the housing complex they both lived in later that evening, Ashley walked Cheryl to her door and they chatted briefly. He really wanted to kiss Cheryl there and then, but as a shy boy, he felt a little intimidated. Then, he surprised himself by asking, 'Can I kiss you?' Cheryl dissolved into laughter and teased, 'Who says "Can I kiss you?",' as she revealed in her engagement interview with *OK!* magazine a year later.

From then on, the couple were inseparable, practically moving in together, and enjoying many intimate nights at home, watching TV and cooking meals. To start with, Cheryl and Ashley were keen to keep their relationship under wraps so they could take things slowly and get to know each other a little better, but soon Cheryl decided she was ready to make it serious.

'We'd both recently come out of relationships and we wanted to start out as friends and get to know each other,' Cheryl recalled in *OK!*, 'but we got to the point where I thought, "I just don't want to meet someone else." I was kidding myself by playing it cool, so I said to him one day, "I don't want us to see other people."'

It was during one of their nights in front of the TV that Ashley melted Cheryl's heart by blurting out the 'L' word for the first time. Cheryl was stunned. She recalled in *OK!* magazine: 'I was making him laugh, pulling faces and doing silly voices. You know when you say something before your brain's even thought about it! His face went green, it dropped a mile. He looked scared. I was pissing myself laughing. Howling. Then later I texted him to say I loved him too.'

It wasn't long before word got about that Cheryl and Ashley were an item. The pair were spotted dancing at London's Funky Buddha club, just hours after Cheryl had flashed her smile at the National TV Awards. According to partygoers the pair were very close all night and couldn't keep their hands off each other.

While Cheryl's bandmates were thrilled that she had

found a good man, Ashley's teammates had a ball taking the mick out of him. In his autobiography, Ashley recalled how at training, he would saunter back into the dressing room and find sexy pictures of Cheryl stuck to his seat, while Jens Lehmann kept joking that he was waiting for the day Ashley recorded a duet with his new girlfriend, even though he was tone deaf. Dennis Bergkamp was the worst. While Ashley was being tended to in the treatment room, Bergkamp would be lying back reading a copy of *Loaded* or *FHM* and start groaning and saying, 'Look at this woman.' Of course the picture would be of Cheryl and Bergkamp would pretend that he hadn't seen Ashley.

But Ashley didn't take the banter to heart, it was all part of being in a football team, and he loved it. He particularly loved it because he knew that in spite of all the jokes hurled in his direction, he was the lucky guy going out with Cheryl. The rest of his teammates were just envious.

While the pair's first public appearance was a paparazzo's photo of them heading to the cinema near Bluewater in Essex in December 2004, the couple were properly outed a few days later when Cheryl attended Ashley's twenty-fourth birthday party at Tantra club. Unsurprisingly, the minute Cheryl stepped out of the car, the paps went into overdrive, especially when some eagle-eyed shutterbug noticed the big sparkling ring on Cheryl's engagement finger. While the tabloids would have a field day speculating about whether marriage was on the cards already, a spokesperson laughed off the suggestion. But if the world needed any more proof that Ashley and Cheryl were a hot couple, it came when a guest rolled up to the party clutching a huge painting of the pair.

So, as the year neared its end, Cheryl's hope for a great 2004 had been realized. Not only had she met the man of her dreams, her career was accelerating beyond her wildest aspirations.

Meanwhile, back at work, following the success of their album, *Sound of the Underground*, the band had been offered a hugely flattering – and humbling – opportunity: to record the single for 2004's Children In Need appeal. Their management hadn't wasted any time in agreeing and the girls were happy with the song choice of 'I'll Stand By You', which was a hit for The Pretenders in 1984. This would be their first proper ballad and they were excited. Not only was it a remarkably different sound for them since it didn't feature any of the traditional Xenomania crazy sounds, they were also convinced it would show a softer side to the band and give their voices a chance to shine – as well as being for a worthy cause close to their hearts.

'All our songs have been up-tempo and quite dancey,' Cheryl said, 'and we just wanted to do a really beautiful ballad that shows off our voices and just shows ... that we can actually sing a slow song – and that we can actually sing.'

When the single was released on 21 November 2004, the girls were ecstatic when midweek figures showed that they were set to oust U2 from the top spot and had left Destiny's Child lagging behind them. They couldn't believe that they had reached number one again, with the single selling almost 60,000 copies in its first week. Surely this boded well for the upcoming album, *What Will the Neighbours Say?*

When it finally hit the shops on 29 November, the girls weren't prepared for what was to come next. The critics' praise for the last album had been exceptional and the girls knew that they'd have to come up with a brilliant album to garner as much, if not more, praise than before. But when they heard what the critics had to say they couldn't believe their ears.

One critic described their songs as 'witty, exuberant and ground-breaking', and the *Telegraph* branded the album 'a glorious piece of pop trash'. Caroline Sullivan, in her *Guardian* review, went as far as to compare the album to the works of Blondie, suggesting it sounded like a 'baby punk version of *Parallel Lines*'.

And the praise was justified. Back to back, the fifteen tracks played like a greatest hits in the making. Highlights included the thunderous 'Wake Me Up', the gorgeous ballad 'I Say A Prayer For You' and the mind-bogglingly brilliant 'Grafitti My Soul'. The latter song had a history: originally penned by Xenomania for Britney Spears after she reportedly told her label she wanted a song that sounded like 'Sound Of The Underground', her people eventually came back to Xenomania, telling them it didn't have a chorus. What was Britney's loss was Girls Aloud's gain because the song is a fan favourite, though it was never released as a single.

Despite all the good reviews, the album only debuted at number six, no doubt because it was battling for space in the Christmas market. But the sales were brilliant, shifting just over 85,000 copies in one week. The album would eventually go on to sell over 600,000 units and be certified double platinum!

On a high, the girls gave their fans another treat: after the disappointment of 2003's cancelled joint tour with One True Voice, the girls were proud to announce that they were to tour the country in the summer of 2005, kicking off in Nottingham. 'We've been itching to do this for a long time,' Cheryl said. 'But we decided to wait until we had two albums' worth of songs to perform before we took to the stage. The time is right for us to give the fans a show they deserve. We're so excited.'

As 2004 drew to a close, Cheryl was happy with her lot. She had her man, her career – what more could she ask for? But over the next twelve months, there were plenty of surprises in store for her.

Chapter 15
GIRLS HIT THE ROAD

The new year kicked off with just as much excitement as had seen out the previous one: more dates were added to their upcoming Summer 2005 tour to feed the fans' demand for tickets, and the girls also discovered that they had been nominated for a BRIT Award. They couldn't believe their luck, though they knew they had stiff competition as they were sharing the Best Pop Act category with pop heavyweights Westlife and McFly.

Things were going so well career-wise that it would have taken a lot to remove the smile from Cheryl's face. Or perhaps that had something to do with the fact that she was blissfully happy with her new man . . .

Since Cheryl and Ashley had gone public with their relationship, the press had become more of an issue in their lives. While this was nothing new to Cheryl, having been exposed to the celebrity media via *Popstars: The Rivals*, young Ashley found it a hard transition to deal with. He knew that a footballer-pop singer combo was tabloid gold. David and Victoria Beckham had proved that the tantalizing combination of a girl songstress hooking up with an athletic sportsman and enjoying the high life was the kind of stuff everyone wanted to read about. But he had never thought he would be part of that circus himself. Before Cheryl he had been dating his ex-girlfriend Emma Barratt for five years and had maintained a low profile. But the minute he started seeing Cheryl, it all changed; the world seemed to go mad and he found himself no longer on the back pages of the papers, but on the covers instead.

When Ashley started out as a footballer, he never imagined himself becoming a celebrity: that wasn't the point of what he did. He wanted to play the sport he loved so much in the best way he could, and one day to represent his country internationally. And he had managed to do it, so far, without the press snooping around. But now it was a different story. Now he wasn't just Ashley Cole, Arsenal midfielder, he was Ashley Cole of 'Cheryl and Ashley' fame.

'I didn't get followed before Cheryl,' he said in his book *My Defence*. 'The press weren't bothered about me. It was all about my football and my performances and that was it. But there's no helping who you fall in love with and I wouldn't have it any other way because Cheryl is key to it all. She's the one person who makes sense of all this madness and she's helped me understand it more.'

Nevertheless, he still found the intrusion very hard to deal with and was visibly uncomfortable with the constant attention from the paparazzi. He became aware that everywhere he and Cheryl went, there was a camera being pushed into their faces, while their every move was being scrutinized for cracks in their relationship. What got to him most were the lies that were printed. Even silly stuff such as the time he supposedly went shopping with Mariah Carey in Selfridges. All made up. It also got him down when old girlfriends sold stories about their time together and cast aspersions on his good name. Just a few weeks previously, his ex, Emma Barratt, had claimed in the *Sunday People* that Ashley had cheated on her many times during their relationship.

Of course, Cheryl was used to the downsides of the celebrity lifestyle by now. She knew how to handle the paparazzi – by being cheeky to them. 'She's a tough cookie,' one paparazzo said. 'She'll give you what you want if you treat her nicely, but if you push it too hard, she'll lose the smile and you've lost her.'

At its worst, in the months following her court case with the toilet attendant, Cheryl wanted the press to go away so she could deal with what had happened away from prying eyes. It had been a tough time having snappers sitting in wait for her and trying to catch her off-guard or worse still taking a shot up her skirt. It was at times like these that she could quite easily have given the whole game up. But she loved it too much to do that.

And then, when it was good, when the girls were performing or attending an awards show, Cheryl loved the attention. It was all she had dreamed about when she was young. She had known the pitfalls from early on and she knew that there were many downsides that came with the job. So who was she to complain?

Of course, there was Ashley's footballing life that Cheryl had to adjust herself to as well. When she attended an Arsenal-Chelsea match at Stamford Bridge, she hadn't counted on being reduced to tears by two grown men. Lost in the snaking corridors of the stadium, Cheryl asked two men if they could guide her back to her seat. Instead of giving her directions, the two brutes laid into her.

'This big bald guy suddenly turned on me and started shouting, "Arsenal? ****ing Arsenal? You ****ing Arsenal slag" . . . I was so scared,' she told the *Mirror*. 'I was on my own and didn't know what to do. They were all shouting abuse at me. I just stood there in total shock . . . I'd never been to Stamford Bridge before and I don't think I'll be seeing Ashley play there again.' As the year progressed, Cheryl teased the press by hinting at where her relationship with Ashley was going. 'We've spoken about marriage,' she told the *Sun*, sending tabloids and celeb weeklies into feverish speculation. Were the couple about to get married? Surely not – they had only been seeing each other for a few months. Wasn't it too soon? Yet she declared how seriously she was taking this relationship in the *Sun*: 'I've never been in a relationship like this where I've been treated like a princess.'

But whispers of weddings were forgotten when Girls Aloud attended the 2005 BRIT Awards in February with the hope of claiming a prize before the night was out. But the *CD:UK* viewers chose McFly as their winners and Girls Aloud went home – after a wild night at the aftershow party – empty-handed.

Dusting themselves off after that disappointment, the girls continued their rule over the charts and celebrated the release of 'Wake Me Up' at G-A-Y once again. As always, their fans came out in force to watch them strut their stuff. But this time round it appeared there wasn't as much of Girls Aloud to go around as before. According to reports, record bosses were concerned that the girls were looking a little too thin; this, coming almost a year after the same people had supposedly ordered the girls to burn off the pounds. Louis Walsh said he thought they were way too thin and declared in the *Daily Star*, 'The problem is everyone's telling them how good they look.'

Cheryl laughed off the worries about their weight, saying, 'All these magazines say we're too big one minute and too thin the next. What are our fans supposed to think? I think these magazines are irresponsible to go on about people's weight so much.'

Cheryl also had a bee in her bonnet about press speculation that she had had a breast augmentation. Rumours had been circulating since she had worn a particularly tight-fitting dress earlier in the year – and Cheryl wasn't happy about it.

'I'm furious about these rumours,' Cheryl told the *Mirror*. 'My dad called me and said he'd seen my picture on a show about celebrities and plastic surgery in which they compared me to Jordan and Jodie Marsh. I've never had my boobs done. It's so upsetting. It's not my fault they're pert . . . I'm sure in years to come, after I've had kids, they'll be down by my knees, so I'll probably need some help then. But at the moment they're all my own. See, no scars in my armpits nor on my boobs.'

Meanwhile, with money pouring in, Cheryl revealed she wanted to open a tanning salon, and was reported in the *Sun* and *Daily Star* as saying, 'I've paid off my mum's mortgage but I really want to buy a tanning salon. It will be a great little family business and we will call it Tweedy's Tanning.'

Unfortunately, before she could set about putting her plan into action, Cheryl was distracted by an offer to present Saturday morning music show *CD:UK* with Dave Berry. Cheryl had never really considered presenting before, since singing was her first love. She was a little apprehensive, but, always one to take on a new challenge, she threw herself into it wholeheartedly.

However, when she was standing on stage next to Dave, she began to wish she'd never agreed to do it. Reading an autocue and making sure she finished in time to cut to an act or video was confusing, especially with producers speaking in her earpiece. But Cheryl soon relaxed and took to the job like a duck to water. Producers were thrilled with her, and rated her performance on the show highly.

'She was a natural in front of the cameras,' one studio hand at *CD:UK* said. 'Once she got past her nervousness, she came into her own and provided a great foil to Dave's witticisms. It's not easy presenting a live show like that and she did it brilliantly. If the band ever folds, she can always try TV!'

Although she was critical of her performance, once she'd come off set, she decided that she hadn't been so bad after all. 'I was absolutely shitting myself,' she said. 'I enjoyed it but people don't realize how hard it is. I'm not saying I'd never do it again, but I wouldn't look for a career in it.'

By April, changes were afoot in the Girls Aloud camp. With Louis Walsh taking a step back, the girls welcomed legendary manager Hillary Shaw into their lives. A glamorous and formidable woman, Hillary had made her name managing eighties girlband Bananarama. At that point she was also looking after Girls Aloud's old rival Dannii Minogue.

When rumours started to circulate that Hillary's appointment was part of a plan to oust him from his position, Louis revealed that he was actually behind Hillary's hiring, explaining that she would be looking after the day-to-day running of the group. 'We have open discussions about the future of the band and we know where we stand,' he said.

Of course that didn't stop him from inspiring more headlines when he worried fans by announcing that he hoped to manage Nadine when she went solo. 'I've never made it a secret that I would like to manage Nadine one day,' he told the *Sun*. 'She is one of the most talented girls I have ever worked with.' Fans, panicking that their favourite group was heading towards an end, were reassured by the label, who said there were no plans for the band to split or Nadine to go solo. Cheryl, irritated by the reports, stated: 'What sane person is actually going to want to leave the biggest girlband in the country? The story is just rubbish. We are working incredibly hard and nobody is leaving the band. Although we have been around two years we feel like we are just starting out.'

She also explained that the greatest hits that was in the works and would follow their third album was merely contractual and was not an indicator that the girls would go their separate ways.

However, that didn't slow down the number of split stories that made the headlines. The *Sun* columnist Victoria Newton predicted the band would last just a year, while Cheryl's stint on *CD:UK* had inspired some creative news writing that she was about to jump ship to become a full-time telly host.

Meanwhile, Cheryl was pleased to hear that she had shot up to number two on the *FHM* annual '100 Sexiest Women in the World' list. And it was a good year all round for the girls as Sarah had jumped to number eight, Nadine was number thirty-five, while Kimberley and Nicola were new entries at forty-four and seventy-seven respectively.

But the girls didn't pat themselves on the back for too long: they had a tour prepare for. After weeks of rehearsals, they began their jaunt with a pre-tour warm-up gig in Rhyl on the Welsh coast and went down a storm with their fans. When they emerged on stage for their first number, 'The Show', Cheryl knew they had finally arrived. Sure, they had played to packed houses before, but usually only at roadshows or on clubnights where the band were only part of an evening's entertainment. This was the first time they had specifically asked fans to come and see them, and they had done so in their droves. Looking out at the sea of faces and arms waving in the air was amazing for Cheryl. As she glanced at her bandmates, she knew they'd come a long way: this is what they had worked so hard for.

Afterwards, Cheryl couldn't contain her excitement about their first night on tour. 'It was so overwhelming,' she enthused. 'It was amazing seeing the people that have made you who you really are, bought your albums, supported you the whole way through and you're giving them something back – bouncing off each other.'

It wasn't just the fans who loved the show – the critics did too, just as they had the band's albums. Girls Aloud, it seemed, could do no wrong.

When they reached Dublin in June the tour was at an end, and no sooner had they stepped off stage after their closing song, 'Sound Of The Underground', than the girls dashed to the city's Lillie's Bordello club for their end-of-tour party. It was the first time in weeks that they were able to relax with their family, friends, dancers and crew without worrying about hangovers the next day.

Cheryl was particularly excited that Ashley had flown out for the final night. She had missed him on tour but she made sure that they either spoke or texted messages of love every night. And now he was there with her. 'We're madly in love,' she told the *Mirror* at the gig. 'I think he's gorgeous. His football season is over now and Ashley flew over to Dublin to see our last show. We're on two weeks' holiday after this. We're all going away on sunshine holidays with our boyfriends. The exact locations are being kept a secret.' Cheryl's own particular 'sunshine holiday' turned out to be a vacation she would never forget.

Chapter 16
SANDSTORM PROPOSAL

When Ashley and Cheryl touched down in Dubai, it felt as if they were in another world. The sun was high in the sky and the heat was ferocious, but better still they hadn't been met at the airport by any paparazzi. For the first time in a long while they both felt free and finally able to relax and enjoy the world a little without worrying about someone jumping out in front of them and taking their picture.

Ashley was particularly pleased about that because this trip to Dubai wasn't just a holiday: he was going to ask Cheryl to be his wife. Ashley was nervous, but in a good way. He and Cheryl had only been seeing each other a few months, but he knew that she was the girl for him and he couldn't imagine being with anyone else but her.

Four weeks before the football season had ended, Ashley went on the hunt for a ring and found one that he was sure Cheryl would fall in love with – a single champagne diamond ring that reportedly cost around £50,000. When he had bought the ring and put it away for safe keeping, he was flushed with excitement. He couldn't wait to ask his girl to marry him.

The plan was that Ashley would take Cheryl on an intimate safari trip. After a short camel ride, he would sit her on a sand dune, whip out a bottle of champagne, produce the ring and then ask her to marry him, all as the sun was setting. It was simple, it was romantic and he knew she'd love it.

Unfortunately for Ashley, things didn't run as smoothly as he had hoped.

Just as they were preparing to set out for their safari jaunt, a ferocious sandstorm whipped up from nowhere. Rain began pelting against the windows and strong winds howled around them, uprooting their wooden sunbeds and creating sand twisters. Ashley and Cheryl couldn't believe what was happening. This was supposed to be a romantic getaway in the sunshine, and now it felt as if they were spending a wet weekend in Skegness. Ever resourceful, Ashley excused himself from the room, leaving Cheryl standing mesmerized by the stormy scene outside. Tucked away in the toilet, Ashley decided the time was right to ask his prospective father-in-law permission to marry his daughter. He was determined to do it by the book, which meant calling Cheryl's dad.

As he waited for Garry Tweedy to answer his call, Ashley grew nervous. When Garry picked up, Ashley said, 'Hi, it's Ashley Cole. I want to ask for your permission to marry your daughter.' There, he'd said it. It was out there and there was no going back. Thankfully, Garry was only too pleased and gave Ashley his seal of approval.

Returning to Cheryl, Ashley discovered that the storm had stopped just as fast as it had started and the sun seemed even hotter than before. So off they went, melting in the heat, to find their guide for their safari trip. But when they did, Ashley was alarmed to discover that the intimate trip was nothing of the sort and that they'd have to share their very romantic experience with ten other holidaymakers.

While he fretted over his scotched plans, Cheryl, who was clinging on behind him on their camel, was having a nightmare herself because she was worried about the welfare of the camels they were riding. Ashley recalled the farcical scenario in his autobiography, *My Defence*, with Cheryl whispering, 'Ashley, I think this is cruel, these poor cute animals dragging us big lumps around in this heat. Their nostrils must really hurt. I'm telling you, when we climbed on I'm sure I heard the camel groan.' Frustrated that his plans had been ruined, he snapped back, 'It's a camel, Cheryl. Camels groan.'

She wasn't having any of it. 'What if he is suffering? What about his feet treading through all those prickly bushes?' Ashley couldn't take any more and, without thinking, yelled, 'Babe! Is there any chance you can shut up?'

From that moment on Cheryl refused to speak to him. What a proposal this had turned out to be. Halfway through the camel trek, Ashley decided that even though it hadn't worked out the way he'd wanted it to, he was still going to do what he'd come here for. As the sun started to set, he pulled Cheryl off her camel, sat her down on the sand dunes and brought out some champagne and strawberries he'd brought along. That worked a treat and Cheryl let a smile appear on her face. Ashley knew it was now or never, even if she was still mad at him for shouting at her.

As the sky grew darker, Ashley turned to Cheryl and asked her to stand up. When she did, he knelt in front of her. She looked down at him, her dark eyes smiling. She knew what was about to happen and she couldn't believe it. Ashley prepared to launch into the big speech he had planned back in London. But as he tried to remember his first line he knew it was futile. He was so choked up that he could barely say a word. Finally, clearing his throat, he managed to say, 'I love you. Will you marry me?' In an instant, Cheryl said 'Yes' and the couple fell into a warm embrace. The holidaymakers around them guessed what had just happened and gave them a round of applause.

On the way back to their villa, the pair talked about their big day, and laughed about the fact they were going to get married. Who would have thought it? The two of them getting hitched after such a short time? But it was happening. And if Cheryl couldn't believe it, all she had to do was look at that big diamond ring sparkling on her finger for proof. And to think – if it hadn't been for that psychic back in Newcastle, none of this might ever have happened.

Chapter 17
LIVING DOLLS

When Cheryl and Ashley flew back home, the press had a field day. As they strode through the airport arm in arm, no one could miss the big diamond ring on Cheryl's dainty digit.

The rest of the girls were over the moon about the news and couldn't wait to congratulate her on being the first Girls Aloud member to get engaged. 'They are so perfect together,' Kimberley said at the time. 'They are so similar. They make each other laugh and they are both so beautiful. They are made for each other.' Nadine was straight on the phone to them, saying, 'I can't believe you are getting married – you've grown up!'

The couple officially announced their engagement in *OK!* magazine. It was a tough decision for both of them to make as they would have preferred to have kept the ins and outs of their engagement to themselves. But they knew if they kept the details of their lives too private they would merely encourage the press to snoop even more. 'By telling the story of our engagement to *OK!*, we ensured that the truth was out there, in our own words,' Ashley explained in *My Defence*. 'Life has become a balancing act between maintaining our privacy, keeping the press happy and handling the stories as they happen.'

In the interview, which took place at Ashley's gorgeous home, the couple opened up about how they met and how Ashley had proposed. Cheryl cheekily poked fun at the way Ashley had announced himself on the phone to her dad.

'He thought it was a joke,' she giggled in her *OK!* engagement interview. 'Who rings their girlfriend's dad and says, "Hi, I'm Ashley Cole." My dad thought it was a wind-up!'

Cheryl went on to reveal that she wanted to have a big fairytale wedding, complete with horse and carriage, but hadn't decided yet whether or not her bandmates would be bridesmaids – 'I'll have lots, but there is a lot of family.' She also spoke about how happy she was with Ashley and admitted that she was thrilled to have her dream job and her dream man, and that eventually she'd like to introduce at least five children into their lives.

Cheryl's joy was slightly clouded due to a spat with Charlotte Church, who, Cheryl said on Radio 1, was 'using our [Girls Aloud's] sound' for her move into pop with the single 'Crazy Chick', sparking an argument that would last for months. The *Mirror* reported that the Welsh wonder hit back and challenged Cheryl to a sing-off at the *Glamour* magazine awards, saying, 'As soon as you can sing "Ave Maria", then you can have a go!' Charlotte added: 'I used to love Girls Aloud but not any more after that. Girls Aloud wouldn't be able to sing "Crazy Chick" if they tried. They just don't have the range.'

The argument continued when Cheryl criticized Charlotte's Walkers Crisps television advert, saying it was appropriate that she was seen to be stuffing her face with crisps. She also commented in the *Sun* that she thought Charlotte's hunky rugby-player boyfriend, Gavin Henson, was a 'posing idiot who looks like a girl'. This was like a red rag to a bull for Charlotte, who hit back: 'I thought it was funny to start with, but now it's just pathetic and I'm going to knock her out if I ever see her.'

Thankfully, a truce was finally called and Cheryl said in *The Times* that the whole argument had just been a misunderstanding. 'Someone asked me if I was devastated we hadn't recorded "Crazy Chick". I just felt like it was an insult because we had good records. I said, "We're moving on now, so if Charlotte wants to do that sound she can." . . . We've yet to kiss and make up, but I'm open to the idea.'

Schoolgirl spats weren't all that occupied Cheryl's mind. She and Ashley were rattled when they discovered that a gang was plotting to steal her £50,000 engagement ring. Cheryl was terrified because she couldn't be sure what lengths the gang would go to in order to get their hands on her treasured ring. There were so many stories about people who had been held hostage, or worse, just so a gang could get their hands on some expensive jewellery. 'The whole thing has been pretty scary,' she said at the time. 'I don't really know what is going on and neither does Ashley. It's scary. I am not wearing my ring.' But once the gang had been thwarted, Cheryl declared that if anyone had tried to mug her she would have hit them in the face with her shoes, adding, 'They're scum, picking on a young girl.'

Back at work, Cheryl and the girls were gutted when their next single 'Long Hot Summer' entered the chart at number seven – comparatively low for them – selling just 18,541 copies.

Had the bubble burst? Or was the song not up to scratch? Eighties popstar Phil Oakey from the Human League decided it was his turn to take a pop at the girls, dismissing them as 'a bunch of page-three girls who release songs, not for musical reasons but as souvenirs'. However, the girls didn't really think anything of his comments, as they didn't actually know who Phil Oakey was.

As a result of her relationship with Ashley, Cheryl had now been awarded the label of 'WAG'. And now that she was set to become a footballer's wife, no one was surprised when she announced that Victoria Beckham had taken her under her wing and had promised to take her shopping. The pair had met at a recent England match and Cheryl later admitted that on that day she had learned a harsh lesson if she wanted to be accepted by the other wives and girlfriends of footballers.

'It was so embarrassing. All the girls were really glammed up, then I walked in with chipped nail varnish and wearing a jumper,' Fametastic.com reported Cheryl as saying. 'I think I looked terrible. But Victoria was down to earth and welcoming. She's going to take me shopping in Madrid. I'd love her to style me because she always looks fantastic. I don't know how she does it with three sons. I look up to her.'

Cheryl had always been an enthusiastic supporter of Victoria. When the Rebecca Loos scandal broke back in 2004, she was right there fighting in Victoria's corner in *Top of the Pops* magazine. 'Why doesn't she [Loos] just shut her mouth. She's a scheming bitch – she knew what she was doing and I hope she's proud of herself.'

Of course, because Cheryl and Ashley came from the same professions as Posh and Becks as a singer and a footballer, they had to deal with the press referring to them as the 'new Beckhams', a tag both she and Ashley hated. 'We get fed up with that,' Ashley said in his autobiography. 'It's such rubbish and we don't really know what it means. It's something made up by lazy journalists who want an easy ride.'

He also went on to explain that he and Cheryl looked at the Beckhams as a model couple living in this media madness. 'They've proved a lot of people wrong about the strength of their marriage . . . But seeing what has been thrown at them serves as a warning to the likes of me and Cheryl. David is right when he keeps saying that as long as he has his wife and his boys around him, nothing can touch them. It's how Cheryl makes me feel.'

As time went on, more and more people began referring to Cheryl as a WAG, and she wasn't happy about it. As far as she was concerned, a typical WAG was a girl who had no job, no money and merely lived off her football boyfriend's fortune.

'The label really makes me angry,' she said in *AXM* magazine. 'When people say footballer's wife they think of someone who just goes out shopping with her husband's money. Well, I've got my own career and my own money. It would upset me if anyone thought I was the sort of person who lives off my husband. It goes against everything I was brought up to believe in. It would really make me sick to be kept by somebody!'

Meanwhile, as the girls started work on their third album, *Chemistry*, Cheryl began to think about how her big day would shape up. She checked her diary to see when it would be best to get hitched. It wasn't a hard choice as the following year's diary was already pretty full. There was a three-week window in July 2006 that looked promising, coming after the girls had completed their *Chemistry* tour and Ashley had finished up at the World Cup in Germany.

After a brief conflab with Ashley, the couple decided that they would tie the knot on 15 July 2006 at Highclere Castle in Berkshire, a gorgeous stately home that really conjured up that fairytale feel that Cheryl was looking for. They viewed the building and Cheryl fell in love with it as she strolled through the corridors that boasted so much history, and decided to book it there and then.

Finally it looked as if everything was coming together. Already they had a date set and a venue, and with wedding planners Banana Split on board nothing could go wrong. But then they were dealt a blow. It was 10 September 2005 and Ashley was lying on his bed flicking through the TV channels when he came across a report on the wedding of Katie Price and Peter Andre, which was taking place that day. As the report cut to an aerial view of the couple's top-secret venue, it suddenly dawned on him that they were getting married at the very same location he and Cheryl had chosen. Ashley recalled in his autobiography how he grabbed his phone and called Cheryl's number – he knew she was not going to be happy.

'You're not going to believe this,' he said when she answered, 'but Peter and Jordan are getting married at Highclere today.'

Cheryl's reaction was as he'd expected: 'Right, Ashley, we're changing venues!'

It wasn't that she didn't like Katie and Peter: on the contrary. Sarah Harding was good friends with the couple and they seemed lovely. What worried Cheryl most was that she wanted her day to be special and unique and not compared to anyone else's. If she and Ashley got married at Highclere, people would forever remember that it was the place where Jordan and Peter got married first – and that would never do.

Luckily, the folks at Banana Split were able to come up with an equally stunning option – Wrotham Park, a large and beautiful mansion in Hertfordshire set in acres of greenery. It was gorgeous – so much so in fact that it had been used many times as a location in films such as *Peter's Friends* and *Gosford Park*. What more could a bride and groom ask for?

As autumn drew to a close, the girls decided that they wanted to branch out from singing, and in early November they unveiled their very own range of Barbie dolls. Looking just as polished and perfectly formed as the real girls, their plastic likenesses were perfect keepsakes for devoted fans. Each was individually dressed by the girls. Cheryl chose a crop-top, jeans and a white jacket and was pleased with the result, joking that she thought her doll was too good-looking to be her. Cheryl's doll sold out at toy stores all across the North East, leaving thousands of little girls disappointed on Christmas Day.

Following the comparatively disappointing performance of 'Long Hot Summer' in the charts, the girls' next single, 'Biology', released in February 2006, put them back on the map and entered the charts at number four. It was their tenth consecutive top-ten hit, matching the Spice Girls' record. The album *Chemistry* followed swiftly and once again proved to be a critical success. The girls were particularly pleased because on this album they had given their all and they seemed to be growing each time they released a new album.

Cheryl gushed: 'A lot of pop acts make a big splash with their first album and then fade away. We've done things the other way round. Our albums have got better and better. If we weren't here, people would be crying out for a group like us.' What pleased the girls most was that the critics saw that instead of playing it safe as so many bands before them had done, Girls Aloud were trying to push the boundaries of pop.

The Times was particularly impressed by the new record, saying: 'It's as though Brian Higgins and his team have set out to flout the rules of pop. If it didn't have *FHM* cover stars singing on it, the wah wah nausea of "Swinging London Town" would sit happily between Mirwais and Vitalic.'

The album entered the chart at number eleven, their lowest chart entry, but sold a whopping 81,962 copies in its first week, which would have been enough to have landed them a number one earlier in the year. But the girls weren't fazed. It was close to Christmas and at that time of year, the charts were always filled with greatest hits and compilation albums, so they raised a glass of mulled wine to the phenomenal sales instead.

The girls ended their year by releasing another single, a cover of Dee C. Lee's 'See The Day'. It was a brave move by the record label, as it came just a handful of weeks after 'Biology'. But their label bosses had a canny plan. They wanted to show the diversity of the *Chemistry* album – the wild and crazy pop anthems and the softer, more soulful sound of the band's voices.

And the trick seemed to work as the single entered at number nine – impressive for a Christmas chart full of novelty records – and kept sales of the album buoyant. However, overall, the album wouldn't shift as many copies as the previous one. 'The *Chemistry* album was a great collection of pop songs, no mistake, but this time round something was missing,' a former teen magazine journalist said. '*What Will the Neighbours Say?* had "Wake Me Up", "The Show", "Love Machine", as well as a whole host of great album tracks like "Grafitti My Soul". On *Chemistry* we had to make do with "Biology", which is up there with the best of their tracks, and that's about it. There were one too many ballads cluttering up the album and that's not who Girls Aloud are!'

Was the critical tide finally starting to turn against Girls Aloud? They were about to find out . . .

Chapter 18
FALSE ALLEGATIONS

Cheryl started her 2006 in a dilemma. The wedding was just around the corner and she knew she had to decide who her bridesmaids would be. She wanted to ask her bandmates for sure, as they had been on this journey with her for so long. But if she did that and excluded any family members, she knew there'd be all hell to pay.

'I've got family who will never talk to me again if they're not bridesmaids and my bandmates would probably not forgive me either if they don't get to follow me up the aisle,' she admitted to the *Mirror*. 'But I can't have ten bridesmaids, and I don't want to let anyone down. It's doing my head in, to be honest.'

She didn't let her problem spoil the build-up to the big day, however. 'I'm so excited about getting married,' she said. 'I want a huge meringue wedding dress. It's a tough choice between a fairytale one or a sleek one. I always thought I'd go for something more demure, but this is my big day so I'm going to go for it.'

But choosing a wedding dress was the last of Cheryl's worries when, a few days in to the new year, and during a brief shopping trip to New York with her mum Joan, she received a devastating phone call. Her PR had received a message from the *News of the World* informing him that they were planning to run a story about Ashley having spent the night with a mystery woman on New Year's Eve.

Needless to say, Cheryl felt winded. She trusted Ashley implicitly and knew that the story had to be rubbish, but phoned him to find out where the story was coming from. He reassured her that the story was just lies. Yes, he'd been out with some mates on New Year's Eve, and yes, some girls had latched on to their group, but he had gone home alone. He'd even spoken to Cheryl while he was in a cab heading to a Chinese restaurant, where he ended up enjoying a quick bite to eat on his own. Cheryl was well aware that girls often sold stories about sleeping with celebrities they had in fact never met. She was sure that that was what had happened here and told Ashley that she believed him.

However, Ashley was keen to prove to everyone that he hadn't been unfaithful. To prove his innocence, he instructed his lawyer to speak to the restaurant he'd eaten in and to track down the taxi driver who had taken him there. And he did just that. The restaurant offered up CCTV footage that showed that Ashley had indeed eaten alone and the cab driver vouched that he had picked up Ashley and dropped him off at a certain time – the same time that the girl had alleged Ashley was sleeping with her. Ashley revealed in his autobiography that he was relieved he had cleared his name and was touched that Cheryl had believed in him regardless.

With a great year behind them, there was much talk of the girls potentially being nominated for a handful of gongs at the 2006 BRIT Awards. Theoretically they were shoo-in to scoop the Best Pop Act. After all, as Cheryl pointed out: 'We're keeping pop alive.'

In some ways this was true. Over the past few months, more and more pop bands had fallen by the wayside in favour of singer-songwriters such as the foppish James Blunt. *CD:UK* had been axed, BBC's *Top of the Pops*' future was hanging by a thread and *Smash Hits* magazine had folded after almost thirty years. McFly were still seen as pop but they tried their hardest to compete with the likes of the Arctic Monkeys. Girls Aloud were what they were: pure pop with a kooky twist. Even trendy bands of the moment such as Franz Ferdinand rated the girls: 'There is some good songwriting there,' their frontman Alex Kapranos was reported as saying on MTV.co.uk. 'Out of all the pop acts out there they are by far the best.'

Surely with a testimonial like that, there'd be no question about them winning a gong at this year's ceremony? Wrong! When, in early January, the nominations were announced, the girls were stunned to hear that they hadn't been nominated for a single award. Instead, Kelly Clarkson and Madonna were among the lucky few. The girls were not happy, claiming on ITV2's BRIT Awards show that, 'It's all very American, it doesn't give British pop acts a chance.'

But Girls Aloud didn't have time to wallow for too long because they had to prepare for a trip down under to promote the single. It would be their first time jetting over to the other side of the world and they were very excited about it; although

Result! The girls give One True Voice a kick in the pants as their single 'Sound Of The Underground' trounces the boys' Christmas effort, 'Sacred Trust'.

The future looks bleak as Cheryl appears in court to defend herself against a charge of physical assault in October 2003.

After a troubled year, Cheryl and Nicola kick off 2004 by having a saucy old time at the Astoria nightclub's G-A-Y New Year bash.

Two thousand fans give Cheryl a twenty-first birthday to remember when she and the girls play G-A-Y again in June later that year.

The girls prove they're not just pretty faces by taking home the *Glamour* Magazine Band Of The Year Award 2004.

Cheryl and the girls do their bit for charity by fronting the 2004 Children In Need record, 'I'll Stand By You'.

Girls Aloud kick off their first ever UK tour in 2005 and wow crowds up and down the country with their killer tunes and racy outfits.

Ashley Cole whisks Cheryl off to Dubai in May 2005 for a break, and surprises her with a marriage proposal!

What a doll! Cheryl and the girls launch their own range of Barbie dolls. Unsurprisingly, the Cheryl one sells out across the Tyneside area.

Forget the footie: Cheryl and Victoria Beckham made the 2006 World Cup worth watching when they descended on Baden-Baden to support their men.

Fingers crossed . . . Cheryl and Ashley were criticized for taking part in an advert for the National Lottery.

Wedding of the year! Everyone thought Cheryl and Ashley were getting hitched at Highclere Castle, but Wrotham Park was the real venue for the event on 15 July 2006. The bride arrived in a horse-drawn carriage.

Cheryl proved she could spot a star in 2007 when she gave
X Factor wannabe and eventual winner Leon Jackson
some handy advice – foreshadowing her later role as a judge
on the show in 2008.

Cheryl jets out to Thailand and
then on to LA (*above* at LAX
Airport), heartbroken after
allegations hit the press that
Ashley had cheated on her.

Cheryl returns to the UK in
triumphant style by looking
dazzling at the BRIT
Awards 2008.

Cheryl replaces Sharon Osbourne on *The X Factor* judging panel. She proves a popular choice and, despite rumours that she and Dannii Minogue are at loggerheads, the team (*from left to right: Louis Walsh, Cheryl Cole, Dermot O'Leary, Holly Willoughby, Simon Cowell and Dannii Minogue*) seem to get along well.

A winning trio: Cheryl with her *X Factor* protégée and 2008 winner Alexandra Burke (*left*) and superstar Beyoncé (*middle*) on the night of the final.

The happy couple: Ashley gives his wife a squeeze at the BRIT Awards 2009, showing the world they are back on track.

She's a winner! Girls Aloud pick up a long-overdue BRIT Award in February 2009 – Best British Single for 'The Promise'.

Cheryl, who wasn't a keen flyer, was not looking forward to the long-haul flight.

When they arrived in Sydney, complete with a documentary crew filming their new UK TV show *Off the Record*, an exclusive, behind-the-scenes, six-part documentary series on Girls Aloud for E4, they were pleased to discover that there were barely any paparazzi waiting for them with cameras poised. In fact, when just one snapper approached to take a picture of the girls as they struggled towards their car with their luggage, their faces totally free of make-up, Cheryl asked him politely if he could not take any pictures, and he obliged. 'The paps seem more friendly over here than they are at home,' Cheryl would later say during an interview on morning TV.

Life in Australia was strange for the girls because it felt as if they were back at square one again. A single had been released a few months back, but because they hadn't come out to perform any promotional duties at the time, not many people in Australia really knew who they were. And that meant the girls could hit the town without fear of being snapped by some devilish pap. And that's just what they did, although poor Cheryl found out to her cost that mixing wine and three different kinds of cocktails in one night was not a good idea. The next morning she woke up with more than a headache and was sick outside their hotel. 'I'm not drinking again,' she swore on camera at the time.

Despite their lack of profile, the girls were thrilled when they turned up to morning TV show *Sunrise* to find a gaggle of eager, cheering fans waiting for them and waving banners. 'I never thought anyone would turn up to see us, so it was a welcome surprise,' Cheryl said. 'It's weird to know that people across the world know who we are.'

While their schedule was packed with meet and greets, TV appearances and mini gigs, the girls did get some time off – the highlight of which was visiting the set of *Neighbours* in Melbourne. Stepping onto the famous street they'd grown up watching on TV was surreal for the girls and it made them realize just how far they'd come.

Life was great for Cheryl, as she soaked up the sun and was ferried around Australia like a queen. Work was going brilliantly and she had her wedding to look forward to. What could possibly go wrong?

It was a lazy Saturday evening, after her return from Australia. Cheryl was at band rehearsals, and Ashley was lying on the sofa watching TV when his phone sprang into life. It was Ashley's mum, and she sounded anxious.

She said a taxi driver had told her that he'd just picked someone up from the *News of the World* who had told him that there was going to be a 'gay premiership footballer story breaking tomorrow'. Two names had been mentioned and she thought she should give him the heads up so he could tell his fellow players. Knowing the players who had been named, Ashley got in touch with them straight away to warn them about the story. However, their lawyers had been in touch already. Although his name hadn't been mentioned, Ashley was half convinced that he might actually be one of the footballers named in the scandal: weeks before, his lawyer had been informed that a newspaper was planning to 'do a number on Ashley Cole'.

Ashley recalled in his autobiography how the next morning he and Cheryl dashed to the shop to get their copy of the *News of the World*, to see who was in the frame. Flicking to page seven, they came across the story that was entitled 'Gay As You Go'. Skimming through, the article alleged that two unnamed premiership footballers, referred to as Player A and Player B, were caught on camera indulging in a sexually explicit gay orgy with a friend who was well known in the music industry. According to the report, one of the players was seen putting a mobile phone into his boxer shorts and using it as a sex toy. As there had been talk that a story was about to break on Ashley, rumours circulated like wildfire that he was one of the players, and that his mate, DJ Masterstepz, a Choice FM DJ, was the 'man in the music industry'.

Of course, Cheryl didn't believe a word of it and she told her fiancé that she knew the rumours were rubbish. But still Ashley had been wronged, being singled out for something he had not done.

Things got worse when the *News of the World*'s sister paper, the *Sun*, ran two stories side by side in what Ashley's lawyer claimed was 'innuendo by juxtaposition'. One story, offensively headlined 'Whobummit? Riddle of gay soccer stars', reported that fans were trying to work out who the two players could be. The other was a fluff piece about Ashley and Cheryl, complete with a picture of the couple leaving the Embassy club. At first glance, readers could have assumed the picture went with the 'Whobummit?' story. Ashley wasn't pleased, but Cheryl, upset to see her man so pained, reassured him that no one believed that he would be involved.

Three days later, on Valentine's Day, Ashley and Cheryl were enjoying a romantic dinner. As they were leaving the restaurant, they noticed that there was a lot of paparazzi activity and as they made their way to the car, the paps started shooting at them ferociously. Although Ashley began to grow frustrated with their persistence, Cheryl continued to flash them her brightest smile. In the safety of their car, they both let out a sigh of relief. Cheryl told him not to worry but Ashley recalled later in *My Defence* how he couldn't help but wonder what had got into the paparazzi that night.

They found out the next morning. The *Sun* had written another story and this time, the insinuation was more explicit. 'Ashley's got a good taste in rings,' the headline screamed. Reading further, there were numerous references to the word ring, mobile phones and vibrations.

Ashley recalled in his autobiography that he was so angry he could barely speak. Cheryl begged him to calm down, telling him his lawyers would sort out this sick mess. But Ashley wasn't having any of it. 'Why are they doing this to me?' he yelled. Cheryl didn't have an answer.

He reached for the phone to speak to his lawyer. But it was worse than he thought. The rumours about him and Masterstepz were all over the Internet and were spreading like a virus. All Ashley could think about was what his mum Sue must be thinking right now – or whether Cheryl would start doubting him.

Unfortunately things got worse for Ashley when the *News of the World* took the story one step further with a story headlined 'Numbers up!' Although the footballer and his music-industry pal remained nameless, the newspaper had used a picture that he instantly recognized of himself and DJ Masterstepz, with their faces blurred, out on the town. Ashley was livid and even Cheryl thought this was beyond the pale.

Cheryl stuck by him and Ashley thanked his lucky stars. He knew that some girlfriends would have doubted him straight away and walked out. But Cheryl was devoted to him and he knew she loved him and believed him. As he became more and more upset by the insinuations in the newspapers, Ashley considered giving up the game for good, moving away and living a quieter life with Cheryl.

Ashley's lawyers issued legal proceedings against the newspapers involved, suing them for libel and breach of privacy. In his book, Ashley explained that the breach of privacy proceeding was related to the fact that he was forced to discuss his sexuality with his agent, his lawyer and their assistants. But the action did the trick and the newspapers in question had to issue an apology.

A year later when the dust had settled on the episode, Cheryl spoke to *OK!* magazine about their ordeal for the first time. 'At first I laughed my head off because the suggestion that Ashley was gay was just ridiculous. But Ashley wasn't laughing. It wasn't very nice for any of us. There was a lot of insinuation. It wasn't a good time for him. I just had to be there for him when people said things to him in the street or people asked him if he was gay.'

Asked if she had ever doubted Ashley, Cheryl was adamant. 'Oh God no! I know him. The thing is, the people who say all this negative stuff don't know him at all. He's such a nice, genuine person. He says it doesn't hurt him when stuff is said and he pretends to me that it doesn't bother him, but deep down it's got to hurt him. He's had to get his head around the fact that people will write stuff even if it's not true.'

With the worst of it behind them, Cheryl and Ashley could

now relax and prepare for their upcoming wedding ... But before that, there were the small matters of Ashley taking part in the World Cup, and Cheryl entertaining the nation with Girls Aloud once again.

_____ **Chapter 19**
PLENTY OF CHEMISTRY

With the press's false allegations against Ashley behind them, and with just a few short weeks to go before the wedding of the millennium, nerves began to set in. Speaking at the premiere of *Alien Autopsy* in April 2006, Cheryl revealed that she was feeling really stressed as the big day approached. 'If you ever get married, run away and do it somewhere else,' she advised in the *Mirror*. 'I've hired a wedding planner but all he ever does is call me and ask me to make more decisions. I feel like I'm living with a phone glued to my ear. Right now I'm starting to think I should jack it all in and Ashley and I should run off and elope somewhere. I just want it to be him and me, alone on a beach – but I know my mum would kill me if I did.'

Meanwhile, on the eve of Girls Aloud's E4 documentary series, *Off the Record*, Cheryl revealed she had been helping Ashley keep in tip-top form in the lead-up to the World Cup by giving him a saucy bedroom workout. 'I've been doing my best to help him keep fit,' she told the *Sun*. 'We tackle each other in the bedroom, and he loves me massaging his feet.' She also said that she was definitely going to be in Germany to watch her man represent his country in the World Cup, which conveniently started just as the band's *Chemistry* tour reached its climax: 'I told the other girls at the start that it's an important part of his life and I want to be there for him. I'd love it if he could be with us on tour, but obviously he can't. I've got a couple of weeks off after the tour so I can go and support him at the World Cup.'

Cheryl also said in the *Mirror* that she had cut down on her booze intake. 'I don't really go out much any more – I can't be bothered and I'm not a very good drinker,' she said. 'The other girls can drink me under the table. Sarah is . . . a great drinker and she still always manages to look amazing. If I get drunk at a nightclub I can't bear the pictures of me in the paper the next day.'

Meanwhile, the girls released another single from *Chemistry*, a ballad called 'Whole Lotta History'. Although the girls themselves loved the track and the luscious video, which was shot in gay Paree, the song divided the girls' fanbase. Some believed it showed the most tender side of the band yet, while others thought it was just a bit too wishy-washy and 'Westlife' for Girls Aloud. Nevertheless, the song made the top five, although many believe it was boosted by the B-side track 'Crazy Fool', written by Cheryl with Xenomania, which had proved a hit with fans.

When *Off the Record* finally hit screens in April-May 2006, Cheryl was surprised by what she saw. Although the girls had had a degree of editorial control over what was screened in the show, when she saw it on TV herself she was shocked at the way she came across in certain scenes, especially in one where she was seen swearing her way up a mountainside in Athens. She said on ITV's *This Morning*: 'People said I was complaining all the time, but a lot of it was the way they edited the footage. They make it look like you can only be bothered to climb five steps when you've actually climbed five thousand.'

Rumours of a split blew up again at the end of April when the girls announced that their next album would be their greatest hits. Was the end nigh, as Louis Walsh had previously predicted? Not likely. The girls assured their panicky fans that all was well and none of the girls had any intention of quitting the band for now. Better still, after their greatest hits they could expect another studio album.

But before a 'best of' album was unleashed, there was the small matter of the *Chemistry* arena tour. This was a big deal for the girls. It was going to be spectacular and lot more visual than their theatre tour of previous year, because more money had been ploughed into the staging of the show. And fans weren't disappointed. The outfits were sexier, the routines raunchier and the girls' hair bigger and better than ever.

The set list showcased their best-selling songs. But the girls had one or two surprises up their sleeves, one being a musical medley featuring the songs 'Fame', 'What A Feeling' and 'Footloose', and a rousing rendition of the Kaiser Chiefs' 'I Predict A Riot', which brought the house down. Sadly, the Kaiser Chiefs didn't particularly appreciate their version because Girls Aloud had changed a few lyrics – 'condom' to 'phonecall' in particular – to make them more tea-time friendly.

The critics adored the shows, as did the fans. When the band played Cheryl's home town, the star could barely get through the songs for tears. The reception they received was phenomenal and every time Cheryl's face appeared on the big screens at the side of the stage the crowd would go crazy for their girl next door. During the show she paid tribute to the audience. 'I'm so overwhelmed I can't even talk,' she breathlessly told the ten thousand people who were screaming themselves hoarse. 'I told the girls that you would be the best crowd and I wasn't wrong. This is a dream come true to perform right here in front of my friends and family.' She later commented to the *Sun* that the tour had been amazing and that 'it was like having a party every night'.

With the tour over, and with just a month to go before she tied the knot with her gorgeous man, Cheryl flew out to Baden-Baden, where she and Victoria Beckham would become more talked about than the football matches taking place.

Chapter 20

SUMMER OF THE WAG

During the summer of 2006, the world's eyes were fixed on Germany, where the football World Cup was taking place. But while some were focused on the action on the pitch, the tabloids in the UK were more interested in what the players' girlfriends were getting up to on the streets of Baden-Baden.

It was the year of the WAG and whether the rest of the country liked it or not, the press had become obsessed with what the likes of Steven Gerrard's other half Alex Curran was wearing, or how much Frank Lampard's then-fiancée Elen Rives had shelled out in a boutique on the finest designer wear. Who cared about which footballer was scoring goals, when the guys' more glamorous halves, with their dazzling fashions and wild partying, were attracting more front pages and column inches than the games themselves?

While all the lesser-known WAGs tried their hardest to make an impression on the great British public by strolling around the cobbled streets in massive sunglasses and tiny dresses, the snap-happy paparazzi were keen to get their shots of the big hitters Victoria Beckham and Coleen McLoughlin. But this time round, there was the added bonus of Cheryl Tweedy, making her big tournament debut. Before she had jetted out to Germany, she had felt a little apprehensive, nervous about having to spend so much time in such close proximity to the other WAGs, not just because she'd been critical of the idea of being a WAG in the past, but because she didn't really know any of them and was worried she might feel a little out of place.

She soon lightened up, however, when she discovered on her journey out to Germany that the plane that had been booked for her and some of the other girls was a budget airline, and not a glamorous jet. 'I didn't realize we were flying with Ryanair,' she reportedly joked in the *Independent*. 'I think it's funny. I just hope Ashley has booked us into a nice hotel.'

And luckily for her, he had. Cheryl and the other girls were staying in the ultra-swish five-star Brenner's Park Hotel, which offered its guests all sorts of luxuries and spas. If they so fancied, they could have massages, face and body treatments, take a dip in the plunge pool or clear their pores in the sauna. With all this and much more to choose from, the hotel was the perfect place for a bunch of girls like Victoria and Cheryl, who liked to be pampered.

While Coleen was quite happy to brave the paps and run around the town checking out all the fashion boutiques with the other girls, Cheryl and Victoria preferred to keep a lower profile and enjoy the hotel's luxuries. It wasn't that they didn't want to be with the other wives and girlfriends, as the tabloids had suggested; they just wanted to keep themselves away from the paparazzi.

However, when the girls attended the matches, it was a different story, and Cheryl and Victoria got into the spirit of things. They dressed up in their patriotic colours and enjoyed catching up with the other girls. It was at the first England game against Paraguay that Cheryl got reacquainted with Coleen McLoughlin. They had met a couple of times before at previous matches and once backstage at a Girls Aloud gig in Manchester, but they weren't yet close enough to be called friends. However, Coleen knew that she liked Cheryl. She was funny and had a great way about her so Coleen was hopeful that she'd get to know Cheryl a little better over the next few weeks.

Coleen recalled in her autobiography *Welcome to My World* how, just before the game was about to kick off, she was chatting away with Victoria and Paul Robinson's wife Rebecca in one of the boxes, when she spotted Cheryl wandering around on her own, not really knowing where to go or what to do. Coleen knew how tough it was for a new girl to fit in and she always made sure that the newbies were well looked after. She got Victoria to call Cheryl to join them. Knowing it was Cheryl's first trip away with the girls, Coleen made an extra effort to make her feel welcome and eventually Cheryl came out of herself and relaxed.

'People don't appreciate how hard it is to go to a match for the first time when everyone is in little groups and seems to know one another. It's intimidating,' Coleen said in *Welcome to My World*. 'Everyone made out that Cheryl didn't mix with the rest of us and that she and Victoria hung out on their own together. But that wasn't the way it was. She might not have come out in the evening all the time but we met up and went out for lunch – she's a lovely girl.'

Cheryl dismissed reports of her not getting on with the other WAGs. 'Everything was fine with me and the girls,' she told *OK!* magazine. 'All the girls were lovely to me. I loved Coleen, as well as Victoria. Coleen is so down to earth and she has started to make a career for herself. The thing I like about her is that she and Wayne have been together since school. You know, she didn't quit her job and start to live off his money like some do. They grew up together. But she has ambition and goals. I admire that.'

British tabloid speculation that Cheryl was purposefully keeping her distance from the other girls was just nonsense. She is a private person and her priority on this trip was always Ashley. She was there for him, to support him, not to try to outshine him. Cheryl got to see Ashley on the days after England had played a match, when she and Ashley's mother Sue were allowed to visit him for a short time. These were special days for Ashley, as at all other times the team were pretty much trapped in their own hotel without any contact with the outside world. To see their loved ones, even just for a few hours, was enough to make being cooped up bearable for a few days.

However, there was one night when Ashley was allowed to sneak out of his hotel and enjoy a brief time with his wife-to-be and family – to celebrate his mum's fiftieth. Being the good, loving son he is, he decided to throw her a surprise party and secretly booked a wine cellar restaurant in town for the celebration, where he arranged for the staff to decorate the interiors with banners with the number fifty on them. He recalled in his autobiography how he assigned Cheryl the job of getting Sue to turn up without suspecting a thing, which she did brilliantly. When they arrived at the restaurant, Sue dissolved into tears when she saw the decorations and the wives and girlfriends who had turned out for her.

But the biggest surprise of the night was yet to come. Ashley had managed to persuade Sven-Göran Eriksson to let him leave the hotel for half an hour so that he could go and give his mum a big hug. And when he arrived, his mother was over the moon. It was lovely for Cheryl that amidst all the madness of the World Cup, she and Ashley and Sue were able to enjoy an intimate family moment like this.

And of course it meant a great deal to Ashley to have his family so close to him during this stressful time. Every time he was on the pitch he could look up into the stands to find his family and they would be looking back at him with pride.

'They all lived and breathed that tournament with me,' he recalled in *My Defence*. 'So it was all good to share that surprise with them. I was only allowed to stay at the party for half an hour but it was a good night made even better because the press missed it.'

But those special times, such as Sue's birthday, were few and far between, so Cheryl had to find other things to do. And, as Victoria was the person she knew best, she spent most of her time with her, mainly lounging around their suites and ordering room service.

One night during their stay, Cheryl and Victoria decided they wanted a night out and gave the paparazzi what they'd been waiting for for so long. Dressed to the nines in pencil skirts and frilly blouses, the two glamorous girls, with their long flowing tresses blowing in the evening breeze, tottered precariously in their heels along the cobbled road for something to eat at the local restaurant. It was one of the few times that the girls made such a public outing and the paps didn't waste a single moment. The next day the papers had a field day suggesting Cheryl looked just like a Posh-in-waiting.

However, that was far from the truth. Cheryl wasn't trying to be like Victoria at all: she had her own style and her own mind. She merely admired Victoria for what she had achieved over the years and looked to her as a great example of someone who made things happen. Like Cheryl, the former Spice Girl turned fashion designer was ambitious, but also just a girl next door. 'She's not a typical footballer's wife. She's ambitious, so we have a lot in common,' Cheryl said. 'She's just so witty and down to earth . . . I love Victoria.'

Her days in Baden-Baden had proven one thing in particular to Cheryl, though: she never wanted the level of celebrity that Victoria experienced. From what she saw of Victoria's day-to-day life – beating off paparazzi and having lies written about her – Cheryl could only admire her more, and she wondered how she coped with the madness day in, day out.

'She handles her life really well,' Cheryl told *OK!* magazine. 'People wonder why she never smiles when she's out and about, but it's because she gets criticized from her head to her toes. Literally. They're talking about her hair, her face, how skinny she is, her bunions on her feet. F**king hell, wouldn't you look miserable? But I think her pout is fabulous, anyway! It's intriguing, isn't it? People just never know what's going on in her mind. But when she's with you she just laughs and smiles all the time.'

According to the *Sunday Mirror*, Victoria and Cheryl talked about life in Madrid over dinner, because there were rumours that Ashley had been asked to join David Beckham out in

Spain at Real Madrid. Victoria had allegedly told Cheryl how wonderful life was in Madrid and that she and Ashley would enjoy their time out there in the sunshine, and assured Cheryl that if they were to move out she would put her in touch with the best estate agents, and show her the best places to go and so on.

Cheryl would later reveal, in an interview with Piers Morgan for *GQ* magazine, that it was around the time of the World Cup that Ashley had indeed been approached to leave Arsenal and head out to Madrid after they had married. The offer was substantial and Ashley thought long and hard about the prospect. David Beckham had gone and had proved to be very successful out there and seemed to enjoy life in Spain.

However, Cheryl wasn't so keen on them moving overseas. Selfish as it sounded, she knew that if the pair of them left for Spain, she'd have to give up her career and she just wasn't ready to do that yet. Girls Aloud were doing exceptionally well and were beginning to be accepted as a band and not just reality TV stars. There was simply no way she could give up on her career or give up on her bandmates.

'I've worked hard to get to where I am,' she told Piers. 'We spoke about it at length. Either I would have had to move out there with him and commute or give up my career at a time when we had finally been accepted as a band . . . I almost begged Ashley to sign to Chelsea, not really knowing what that would mean. I didn't realize the extent to which moving from Arsenal to Chelsea would cause so much hurt between the two of us. I stopped Ashley from living his dream playing out there for that team. And he wouldn't have got half as much shit if he had gone there rather than Chelsea. And I blame myself for that!'

Sadly England's hopes of winning the World Cup were dashed when they were knocked out of the competition by Portugal in the quarter-final, and it was back home for the footballers and their WAGs.

Not long after they returned home to the UK, the couple caused controversy when they took part in a photo shoot to promote a new National Lottery game called Dream Number. Dressed in heavenly white, they posed next to a Rolls-Royce with their fingers crossed. The critics were out in force suggesting it was a tacky stunt, but Cheryl brushed off their comments. They were happy with their decision and that's all there was to it.

Meanwhile, Cheryl found out that Lily Allen had written a song called 'Cheryl Tweedy', which she initially took as an honour. In the song, Lily sings that she wishes she looked like Cheryl Tweedy, which Cheryl understandably took as a compliment. 'I am very flattered that Lily's written a track about me,' she said in the *News of the World*. 'But I don't know why she wants to sing about wanting to be as pretty as me as she looks stunning.'

Unfortunately, Cheryl was unaware that the song was actually a little more satirical than she'd thought. Lily later said on her blog: 'I don't want to look like Cheryl. It's tongue-in-cheek, it's meant to be ironic. I don't have anything against her but I think the portrayal of her being the right thing for kids to look up to is wrong. It was a joke that not many people got. Of course nobody wants to look like Cheryl, they just think they do.'

But the gloves really came off a few months later. When Cheryl was appearing on Gordon Ramsay's *The F Word*, the foul-mouthed chef mentioned their spat again and referred to

Lily as a 'chick with a d***'. Even though Cheryl merely repeated what Gordon had said, Lily took offence and launched another scathing attack on Cheryl.

'I know I've said bad things about people in the past but this I mean ... I may not be as pretty as you but at least I write and sing my own songs without the aid of autotune.' She added, 'I must say taking your clothes off, doing sexy dancing and marrying a rich footballer must be very gratifying, your mother must be so proud, stupid b****.'

But petty squabbles with grumpy popstars were the last thing on Cheryl's mind. She had a wedding to look forward to. So while Ashley jetted out to Puerto Banus with his mates for his stag do, Cheryl stayed in London where she, her mum and her mates lived it up at Umbaba, downing – according to the *Daily Mail* – around £800 worth of champagne and cocktails, until the early hours. Cheryl had laid down rules for the girls that when it came to organizing her hen do, the last thing she wanted was some oily stripper rubbing his tush in her face. She had told *OK!* magazine: 'I keep reading about strippers, but I certainly don't want one. I would be mortified.' And just as she'd ordered, there wasn't a stripper or cheesy hen night prop in sight. Of course, the paparazzi were out in full force, so when Cheryl did eventually stagger out into the street to find her car, they were there snapping at her like maniacs.

In the blaze of flashes, Cheryl appeared slightly shaky on her feet, but mum Joan ensured she made it to the car in one piece. Joan had said that while the other revellers were enjoying the booze, Cheryl had tried to pace herself so she didn't end up being sick or making a fool of herself in front of the paps. Sue, Ashley's mum, admitted to having had a ball, too. 'I stayed out with the girls until around 2 a.m. before I headed home,' she told *OK!* 'I had such a laugh and it was very strange being out with the girls and having all these photographs taken. And then I saw them in the paper, and thought it was hilarious. But it certainly looks like everyone had a good time, that's for sure.'

With the stag and hen dos out of the way, all that remained for Ashley and Cheryl was to get married ... and it would definitely be a day they would never forget.

Chapter 21
WEDDING OF THE MILLENNIUM

It was the wedding everybody had been talking about. One of the country's biggest and most beautiful popstars was to marry a Premier League footballer. It was a union made in tabloid heaven.

Ever since David and Victoria Beckham had married back in 1999 at Luttrellstown Castle, a precedent had been set. Celebrity weddings were no longer just small affairs. Nowadays, when a high-profile couple got hitched, they went to town on celebrating their big day. The Beckhams were the first to turn a personal wedding into a world-stopping event when they married in a small chapel with a Robin Hood theme, and later changed into matching purple outfits and sat on thrones.

Following that, Victoria's so-called rival Katie Price – aka Jordan – similarly went to town when she married Peter Andre in 2005. She had worn a pink gown that defied belief and arrived at the ceremony in a pumpkin-style coach. She wanted a fairytale wedding and that's exactly what she got. The public loved it and snapped up copies of *OK!* magazine as soon as they had hit the shelves.

Three days before Cheryl and Ashley's nuptials, newspapers and magazines around the country were all of a dither. As *OK!* had previously secured a deal with the couple, it meant that no other media was allowed access to the wedding. But if the publications were to feed their readers with all the much-sought-after gossip, they needed to get some sneaky info ahead of time.

And that was the predicament in the *Heat* magazine offices, former editor Mark Frith wrote in his book *The Celeb Diaries: The Sensational Inside Story of the Celebrity Decade*. Like most editors across the country at the time, Mark wanted *Heat* to get a piece of the action, so that his hundreds of thousands of readers could gatecrash the party they hadn't been invited to. The only thing was, as the wedding was to take place on the Saturday and *Heat* normally went to press on the Friday, it meant they needed to put together a behind-the-scenes feature without actually being there – and make it look as though it had been written after the event.

One of his reporters had been told by a source that it looked likely that the wedding was due to take place at Highclere Castle, so he dashed off to investigate. When he arrived at the castle, the sight of a huge white marquee erected in the garden suggested to him that he had stumbled across the wedding of the year. Dashing back to the office, he wrote up his findings and handed over his article. Mark was chuffed as it would mean he had a great spoiler for the following Tuesday.

But what he hadn't anticipated was that his reporter had actually got his wires crossed. Just as the mag was about to be put to bed on the Friday evening, Mark received a call from a paparazzo with the news that a fleet of cars had just swept into Wrotham Park in Hertfordshire, and that a certain Ashley Cole was in one of them. Mark went cold when he realized his reporter had made a terrible mistake! In record time, Mark cut references to Highclere Castle and dumbed down the copy so it was a lot vaguer. He admitted in his book that this episode was one of the most embarrassing cock-ups of his career – though he claimed the Coles had deliberately asked Highclere Castle staff to pretend the wedding was still happening there.

Meanwhile, at that very moment in Hertfordshire, miles away from the *Heat* offices, Ashley Cole and Cheryl Tweedy were exchanging vows at Sopwell House Hotel in front of just close family and friends. This wasn't the big wedding they had planned – that was taking place the next day – but due to legal complications over licences, the couple had to marry one day early. But it didn't matter because the following day they would have the grand wedding they'd dreamed of.

Ashley was the man Cheryl had dreamed about for the whole of her life. He treated her like a princess and she was thrilled. Unlike many other celebrities, Cheryl didn't even want to consider signing a prenuptial agreement. 'I think it's disgusting,' she said in *OK!* magazine. 'I could understand if you were ninety-three and you've got billions of pounds and this twenty-four-year-old wants to marry you after a month. But we're a work in progress, we're going to build our married life together, not thinking about what if it ends.'

And to prove how fully committed she was to him, Cheryl had surprised Ashley by getting a new tattoo. Pulling up her hair after the Switzerland-England game at the World Cup she revealed a brand new etching on the back of her neck that read 'Mrs C'. He was delighted with it.

Now that the big day had arrived, the couple were pleased that the press had been sufficiently thrown off the scent to allow them to marry in private on the Friday. Up until then, every newspaper in the land had thought they were still planning to wed at Highclere Castle, so until the morning of the wedding itself, there weren't many paparazzi hanging around the Wrotham Park gates. But by lunchtime, when word spread that the wedding was at Wrotham Park, the snappers had begun to arrive in their droves.

Twenty minutes away from the house, Ashley was getting ready in his room at the Grove Hotel. The room was in chaos, with clothes and hair products scattered all over the place. His groomsmen, Jermaine Wynters, Paolo Vernazza, Jon Fortune and Cecil Talian, and his best man and brother, Matthew, were busy slipping into their suits and teasing their hair into place, while Ashley was becoming more nervous by the minute. On the dressing table sat two Stephen Webster ring boxes – one containing his wedding band, the other Cheryl's. He recalled in his autobiography how he opened the latter and tears welled in his eyes when he saw the eight-carat heart-shaped yellow diamond glimmering in the afternoon sunlight. He was so excited.

At Wrotham Park, Cheryl was in her bedroom with her mum Joan and her bridesmaids, dressed in her Roberto Cavalli-designed Ming-vase-inspired satin wedding dress. Joan couldn't hold back the tears as she looked at her angelic daughter. She had never looked so beautiful, her body wrapped in a bustier that sparkled with sequins, beads and diamanté. Though the style of the dress was similar to the infamous Ming-vase dress

Victoria Beckham wore to one of Elton John's 'White Tie and Tiara' parties, Cheryl said the Queen WAG had nothing to do with helping to choose the dress.

'We just both love the designer and because we are both similar sizes his clothes fit us both like gloves. I just looked at some of the designs Roberto sketched and it turned out to be my favourite as well.'

Her bridesmaids, who did in the end include both family and her bandmates, looked at her in awe. Cheryl looked amazing. They couldn't believe that one of their group was actually getting married, making that life-changing commitment. But they knew that she had found Mr Right in Ashley and that the couple would live happily ever after.

Her bandmates hadn't expected to be chosen as bridesmaids. Cheryl had said before that she had a big family, and they thought she'd rather choose them. So when Cheryl spoke to them individually and told them that she wanted them to play an important part in her big day, they were over the moon. 'Nicola and Kimberley both burst into tears while Sarah and Nadine were just in shock,' she told *OK!* 'They thought I was going to say I was pregnant.'

At 5 p.m., Cheryl's proud father Garry came to lead her down to the horse and carriage that would drive them out of the mansion's grounds to the nearby chapel where she and Ashley would exchange vows.

As they made their way to the chapel, a million thoughts ran through Cheryl's head. Today would be the most important day in her life: she and Ashley would be made man and wife in front of everyone they loved. It was all she'd ever hoped for. Inside the chapel, Ashley was standing at the altar with

Reverend Keri Eynon. Behind him the pews were packed with excited guests and his groomsmen were trying their hardest to make him laugh, but he was too nervous to humour them.

Around 5.20 p.m., the people inside the church could hear a scuffle on the public footpath outside the chapel. Cheryl had arrived. The scene was utter chaos. As the chapel wasn't on private land, the paparazzi were able to gather around the entrance, which had been covered by a white tarpaulin so that none of them could get a picture inside. When the brides-maids' cars drew up at the entrance, the clicking sound of the snappers' cameras was almost deafening, and as the girls climbed out of the cars and ducked underneath the tarpaulin, the frenzied photographers started beating down on top of it, banging the girls' heads. The girls couldn't believe how ferocious the paparazzi were on such a special day. Cheryl managed to follow the girls in unscathed but she too was horrified by their behaviour.

Taking as deep a breath as she could in her dress, Cheryl let her father lead her into the main part of the chapel. *OK!* magazine reported that, as the wedding party started down the aisle, a gospel choir sprang into life singing Alicia Keys' 'If I Ain't Got You'. Tears filled Ashley's eyes as Cheryl came into view. She was a vision, just like a princess. After a few words of welcome, the reverend recited the traditional wedding vows. In place of hymns, the couple decided to have the gospel song 'Sing The Song', 'Amazed' by Lonestar, and 'Ain't No Mountain High Enough'. When they exchanged vows, the couple promised to love, comfort, honour and protect each other. Cheryl, consumed with emotion, could barely get the words out and wiped tears from her eyes.

After they exchanged their rings, the couple's mothers were asked to step forward to light a pair of candles. Ashley and Cheryl were then asked to use both candles to light their own candle – symbolizing the coming together of both families.

As the couple exchanged a kiss, Cheryl's bridesmaids burst into tears.

'I cried,' Nicola recalled in *OK!* magazine. 'When I was watching her get married I was remembering back to when we shared a room during *Popstars*, thinking, "She's my little girl."' Nadine said it looked as if Cheryl was becoming a woman right before their eyes.

When the ceremony was over, Ashley and Cheryl walked back down the aisle accompanied by a rousing rendition of 'Oh Happy Day' sung once again by the gospel choir, and then the joyous couple headed back to the house for the party.

After a champagne reception, the couple took their angel-winged seats at the top table. Cheryl's dad Garry was first on his feet to deliver his speech, and told the room how, on the day he was handed his baby Cheryl, he thought he had been handed an angel. 'It was the proudest day of my life,' he said. 'What I wanted for her was a smart, sensible, reliable partner and I'm delighted that Ashley is all of those things, and I'm delighted to welcome Ashley to our family.' After that, Garry presented Ashley with a Newcastle football shirt with Ashley's name emblazoned on the back.

The guests then tucked in to the wedding breakfast, which consisted of a starter of Dublin Bay prawn and crayfish cocktail, smoked salmon with English watercress, a parmesan wafer and lemon wedges, roasted and grilled vegetables with pesto dressing. This was swiftly followed by a main course of a juicy fillet steak, with fat chips, peas, grilled mushrooms, grilled beef tomatoes, crisp onion rings and Madeira jus.

When the main course was finished and cleared away, Ashley's brother Matthew gave his best man's speech. In it, he said that he was chuffed that his brother had picked him to be best man but added that if he hadn't, there would have been trouble.

Next, Ashley reportedly took the floor and, after making a few jokes about the location, turned to his beautiful bride. 'I'm the luckiest man and proud that Cheryl is my wife,' he said. 'From the day I met her I knew I'd marry her. And now I'm here celebrating a great day in my life.' He went on to honour their mums and presented them with a bouquet each.

After dessert, Cheryl and Ashley headed out to the dancefloor for their first dance. But Cheryl had a surprise in store for her new husband: she had arranged for soul star John Legend – Ashley's favourite singer whom they'd been to see on their first date – to fly over from the States to perform. Ashley couldn't believe his eyes when the singer appeared on the revolving stage. After Legend performed a handful of songs, the guests, including the Sugababes and Jamelia, hit the dancefloor and threw some shapes until the early hours of the morning.

For the rest of the evening, Cheryl mingled with her guests, telling each and every one of them that she was glowing with excitement and was so pleased that she was now officially Mrs Cheryl Cole. She was the happiest girl in the world.

Later in the evening she dashed upstairs, her face aching from smiling so broadly, and changed into her going-away dress, another Roberto Cavalli creation. Returning to the party, she said her final goodbyes and, taking Ashley by the hand, headed off into the night before they jetted out to the Seychelles for their romantic honeymoon.

Chapter 22
GHOSTS, GREATEST HITS
AND POLITICS

After their luxury honeymoon, it was straight back to work for Cheryl. First up was a co-hosting stint on *The Friday Night Project* with Alan Carr and Justin Lee Collins. On the show, Girls Aloud got to exercise their comedy muscles in a series of sketches. 'We had such a great time,' Cheryl told the *Sun*. 'Alan and Justin just had us in hysterics. And we got to try our hands at acting! But we couldn't keep a straight face.'

Shortly after this they performed some one-off summer gigs, including the V Festival. The girls had been nervous about their gig at this world-famous event, fearful that they'd be booed off stage by fans of more 'credible' bands on the line-up. But they were pleasantly surprised that their set, which included all their hits, plus their version of 'I Predict A Riot', went down a storm. 'We were s***ting ourselves thinking people were going to hate us,' Cheryl said afterwards in the *Sun*, 'but the tent we played at was packed and they had to shut it because it was overcrowded. We were playing the same day as Radiohead and Keane. We couldn't believe it.'

In October, the girls unleashed a brand new single, 'Something Kinda Ooh', which would be the lead release from their upcoming greatest hits package *The Sound of Girls Aloud*. The track was an instant smash and fans deemed it by far the best song of their career to date. The deliciously campy tune proved to have mass appeal and smashed into the charts at number three, their highest chart position since 'I'll Stand By You' in 2004. A week later, their album *The Sound of Girls Aloud* hit the shops and was a dream for their fans, as well as those new to their music. Not only were all the hits there to enjoy, there were three new tracks – 'Something Kinda Ooh', 'Money' and a cover of Tiffany's 'I Think We're Alone Now'. And for the fans who had already purchased their hits, there was a limited bonus disc version of the album, which featured some delightful rarities, including, cheekily, a far superior version of One True Voice's career-breaking single 'Sacred Trust', a cover of Blondie's 'Hanging On The Telephone', a live version of 'I Predict A Riot', plus a handful of new tracks such as 'Singapore' and 'Loving Is Easy', plus new versions of 'Sound Of The Underground', 'No Good Advice' and 'Wake Me Up'. The perfect package for devoted fans who lived and breathed the girls. The joyous track list and bonus disc worked their magic on the charts, giving the girls their first number one album, which went on to sell 815,000 copies.

In the lead-up to Christmas 2006, Girls Aloud released another single on 18 December, this time a remixed version of 'I Think We're Alone Now', which was featured on the soundtrack to the film *A Boy Girl Thing*. Also around this time, some of the girls took part in a one-off special for ITV2 called *Ghosthunting with Girls Aloud*. Hosted by Yvette Fielding, it borrowed a format from her own Living TV show *Most Haunted*, only with celebrity guests thrown in the mix to stir up some spooks.

The girls, minus Nadine, who didn't want to mess around with the supernatural, were packed off to disused Crossley Hospital morgue in Cheshire and the seventeenth-century mansion, Plas Teg, in Pontlydyn, Wales. Although they were fearful of fooling around with things they didn't understand, Cheryl admitted that she wanted to find out more about ghosts and ghouls and to see if they really did exist! To some degree Cheryl was a believer. Not only had that psychic predicted her romance with Ashley, she once thought she'd seen a spook of her own.

'I was in on my own at home and my dog started barking,' she revealed in an ITV press release interview. 'He was going mad and I didn't dare look. When I did, it was some smoke! I screamed the place down. I thought it was a ghost because I was terrified.' On the *Ghosthunting* show, the girls' curiosity turned to terror when they started filming. During one of the scenes, Cheryl's most nerve-tingling moment was when she felt as though someone had stroked her arm.

'It felt like someone brushing my arm, like a stroke almost,' she recalled. 'It happened really quickly. It was unexpected and I was really scared. I definitely thought it was something.'

Following the show, Cheryl became convinced that there is life after death. 'I think something definitely exists. The ghosts do seem to go to very old places though.'

And it wasn't only ghosts Girls Aloud were facing up to in December – they were bringing politicians to account in the *New Statesman*. Their controversial interview with the highbrow political magazine was a surprise to their fans – and it was a welcome relief for the band to answer questions about serious subjects and not merely to be hassled about which stars they hated or what was going on in their love lives. In the feature, the girls said they wanted to make politics more user-friendly.

'It just isn't talked about in normal magazines,' Sarah said. 'We never get asked about who we vote for. Everyone has ideas about what we want for the country but people need to vote to make that happen.'

Cheryl agreed. 'Our fans would definitely listen to us,' she said. 'They'd think, "Well, if Kimberley and Cheryl and Nicola are interested in it, then I want to know about it."' She added, 'Politicians know that we get listened to by more young fans than they do. That's why David Cameron said he fancied me. He was just trying to be cool. I bet he couldn't name a single song of ours. Do I fancy him? No! Politicians should stop trying to be cool and get on with running the country.'

She also criticized the WAG culture once again, suggesting that since the heyday of the Spice Girls, the notion of Girl Power was all but forgotten.

'I think that's all gone. When the Spice Girls went, Girl Power went, too,' she said. 'They didn't actually change anything. It's bad really. These days young girls are more likely to aspire to marrying footballers and living luxurious lifestyles. It's the media that puts them in that state of mind ... What kind of aspiration is that? Footballers' wives are just as bad as benefit scroungers – it's just a higher class of sponger.'

Having proved they were more than just airhead popstars, the girls were back to doing what they did best – selling out their forthcoming Summer 2007 Greatest Hits tour: tickets had sold out within days of going on sale, and they were looking forward to starting work on their fourth studio album.

The new year was a lucrative one for the girls. Their manager had brokered deals for them to front a variety of products. Back in 2006, they had signed up to front Coke Zero. In 2007, they had been signed up to front big-money deals for Sunsilk shampoos and, later in the year, for the Purple Samsung phones. Both launches were celebrated with flamboyant bashes.

In February 2007, Cheryl and Kimberley took part in a stylish photo shoot for *OK!* magazine, which was based on an Italian film from the sixties. When the girls saw the finished shots, they were delighted, and the set of pictures, shot by Sven Arnstein, became their instant favourites.

In the *OK!* interview accompanying the shoot, Cheryl spoke for the first time about the gay rumours that had plagued her husband the previous year, and explained that she had dismissed the allegations as silly, but that it had been a tough time for the pair of them. She also hit back at criticism she and Ashley had received for selling their wedding to *OK!* magazine.

'I didn't care,' she said. 'The people who slagged us off were the ones who write nasty, hurtful things all year round. At the end of the day, I wanted my fans to see the wedding as it was. If it wasn't for them I would never have met and married Ashley. I also wanted it to be documented so my kids could see it. I wouldn't do it any differently – I had the wedding of my dreams.'

She also revealed that Ashley was a rubbish house husband. 'He doesn't do a thing,' she laughed. 'Not a thing. Maybe he'll make me the odd cup of tea, but that's it. Luckily my mam lives with us and she'll do lots of stuff. But we're having an amazing time. I love being married.'

In fact, marriage, she said, had changed her and calmed her down and she admitted that she would rather be at home watching the TV and eating a takeaway than being out on the tiles.

In the same article Cheryl spoke out on the shock news at the time that her old *Popstars: The Rivals* mate Javine Hylton had recently been found in bed with pop singer and co-star of the musical *Daddy Cool*, MC Harvey, who was married to singer Alesha Dixon from Mis-Teeq at the time.

'All I know is if it happened to me, the guy would be dead,' she said, not realizing that these words would come back to haunt her a year later. 'Of course, it depends on the circumstances. If everything was happy at home and Ashley did what Harvey did I would shrivel up and die. But if things weren't going well at home it wouldn't come as a surprise . . . Trust is so important to me. I have been cheated on so many times in my past. And when I was I gave the blokes a few rights and lefts.'

In March, the girls were back at work again and recorded a charity single for Comic Relief with the Sugababes. Their track, a cover of 'Walk This Way' by Run DMC and Aerosmith, was an instant hit and went straight to the top of the charts, raising much-needed money for good causes. 'It's a great single and will raise money for people living in really difficult situations here and in Africa,' Kimberley said in the *Sun*.

The girls threw their weight behind Comic Relief, with Kimberley flying out to South Africa to see where the money would be spent. Meanwhile, Cheryl, who had stayed in the UK, donated a pair of shoes that she'd worn in the 'Something

Kinda Ooh' video for auction on eBay to raise money for Comic Relief, and took part in the charity's special episode of *Celebrity Apprentice*.

On the show, which had been filmed the December before, Cheryl was in a team with football manager Karren Brady, fashion guru Trinny Woodall, comedienne Jo Brand and actress Maureen Lipman. In spite of some initial fears, Cheryl enjoyed her experience. 'I would definitely do it again,' she said in the *Sun*. 'We raised over a million pounds, which was the aim.' However, she admitted that the experience wasn't quite a walk in a park. 'It was much worse than the nerves I get when I go on stage because I was completely outside my comfort zone,' she said. 'When I walked in on the first day I felt intimidated. But I knew it was important we raised lots of money for *Comic Relief* so I felt a great sense of responsibility.'

Her performance on the show was so good that Sir Alan Sugar sent her a note to congratulate her, saying if he was to hire anybody from the show it would be her. He later said in an interview with *Zoo* magazine, 'Cheryl Cole was very impressive. Everyone was expecting this dolly bird, but she showed street smarts, determination, and great commitment and very impressive business acumen. She'll go far!'

Her appearance on the show also led to Simon Cowell getting in touch with her to invite her to become one of the judges on *Britain's Got Talent*, but Cheryl, touched by the invitation, declined, believing she didn't have the guts to do it.

'I don't think I can be cruel to anyone, really, and who am I to end their dreams in one go?' she said to the *Sun*. 'I wouldn't become a judge. I don't think I'd be qualified. Who am I to judge other people? I know people think I'm fiery but I think

I'd be too diplomatic. I know what it's like to be on the receiving end of criticism.'

In May, just before the girls' Greatest Hits tour was about to commence, they got their first taste of movie stardom when they shot a scene for the remake of *St Trinian's*, starring Colin Firth, Russell Brand and Rupert Everett. The girls, dressed in school uniforms, had easy roles, playing a band at the school dance, but they loved the experience. 'It was a lot different to filming a video. I had to keep getting told not to look into the camera,' said Cheryl on *The Making of St Trinian's*.

Once filming had wrapped, the girls got down to rehearsing for their Greatest Hits show. This was going to be a spectacular tour and Cheryl couldn't contain her excitement. 'It's our biggest show yet, with all our hits, all our career so far rounded up in one show. If you are a Girls Aloud fan you're going to wet your pants.'

She was not wrong. Kicking off their run of dates in her home town of Newcastle, Cheryl and the girls dazzled fans with barely-there outfits, wild and sweaty dance routines and more smash hits than you could shake a stick at.

During the tour, Cheryl opened up about some of her body woes: 'I'm not happy with my body,' she told *Sunday Magazine*. 'I have to watch my weight and really put myself through it, trying silly diets or doing stupid gym workouts ... When I joined the band I put on a lot of weight and at one point was 9st 7lb. Now I have one day a week when I eat whatever I like. Without that luxury, I'd go crazy!' She also confessed in the same interview that Ashley made her feel sexy and happy – and that they wanted children, though were not in any rush.

In June 2007, when the tour was over, Cheryl and Ashley

got to enjoy some carefree time together when they jetted out to the Sandy Lanes resort in Barbados to celebrate their first wedding anniversary. There, they basked in the sun and made the most of their intimate time away from the grey skies of the UK and the persistent gaze of the paparazzi.

When they got back to their Oxshott home, Ashley had a surprise for Cheryl – a £150,000 Bentley. While Cheryl was amazed by such a gift, she told Ashley that she couldn't accept it. 'It was lovely, but I just couldn't . . . ' she said in the *Daily Star*. 'I have my own Mercedes SUV, and I bought that when I thought I'd worked hard enough to deserve it. I don't feel I've done enough to deserve a Bentley. I'm not one of those girls who goes out and spends £1,500 on a handbag. At the moment the car is just sitting in our drive waiting to go back to the shop.'

But while Ashley was no slouch in the gift department, he was still not pulling out the stops when it came to more domestic roles! 'He's totally pathetic round the house. I've had this discussion with his mum where I blame her, basically,' Cheryl joked to the *Sun*. 'She never made him do anything and they are so well looked after at football, too, that he's spoiled. They don't even want them picking up a heavy suitcase in case they get injured, it's ridiculous. I've tried to help Ashley be a bit better. He's now learned to iron – which is quite impressive for him.'

Cheryl also explained that she is the better cook of the two, and that she finds tidying up therapeutic. However, prophetically, she admitted that she preferred being a homebody because when they went out together girls threw themselves at him. At the time, though, she found it funny. 'I trust him one hundred per cent so I'm not worried about it,' she said in the *Sun*. 'Maybe if I was insecure I would, but I'm not. These girls are sad anyway. I couldn't be one of those footballers' wives who just accept them sleeping around because they live in a nice house and have designer handbags.'

Back at the day job, Girls Aloud next released the ferociously energetic single 'Sexy! No No No ...', at the end of August, which charted at number five, giving them a record-breaking sixteenth top-ten hit in a row.

Their fourth studio album, *Tangled Up*, was released in November 2007, and once again gave the girls a top-ten album, peaking at number four. Yet again, Girls Aloud found themselves a hit with the critics – the BBC labelled the album 'yet another unrelenting pop masterpiece' and called the girls 'undoubtedly the best girlband the UK has ever seen', while the *Guardian* described *Tangled Up* as 'irresistible' – but fans were disappointed by the album sleeve, which had dispensed with the usual picture of the girls and instead just featured the band's logo.

Fans complained on their website forums that the album looked 'cheap' and 'just like those unofficial albums you get in the bargain basement'. Conspiracy theories blew up that the album was released in preparation for the departure of Nadine Coyle. This was hastily denied and the band said that the lack of a picture was due to technical reasons beyond the band's control.

The fans were soon given something to cheer about, however, as a 2008 Girls Aloud tour was announced following the success of their Greatest Hits tour in the summer. And a couple of weeks after the release of *Tangled Up*, the girls released what some fans consider one of their best singles yet, 'Call The

Shots'. A lot more restrained than their usual fodder, but not quite as slushy as previous ballads such as 'I'll Stand By You' or 'Whole Lotta History', the song won high praise from critics, such as Kim Dawson from the *Daily Star* who said it was 'classy electronic Europop with real edge'. The video was shot in Malibu and featured the girls in purple dresses. Some fans thought the heavy-handed inclusion of the purple Samsung phones in the video was a product placement too far, but the quality of the song and its positive reviews helped banish the naysayers.

Prophetically, given her future role on the show as a judge, in December 2007 Cheryl and the girls made a guest appearance on *The X Factor*, to give the wide-eyed hopefuls – including the eventual winner Leon Jackson – some handy advice on singing and how to handle the press attention. And it wasn't the only TV they were working on: as the year drew to a close, the girls started work on their latest TV series, *The Passions of Girls Aloud* for ITV2. Over the next few months, four of the girls – as Nadine felt it unnecessary to take part in a show that wasn't directly promoting the group's musical output – would each pursue a dream they had longed to accomplish. Sarah's was to play polo, Nicola's to create a make-up range for people with pale skin, Kimberley's was to be in a West End musical, while Cheryl wanted to try her hand – or feet – at street dancing. Her pursuit would take her over to America where she would hang out with street dancers, meet choreographers and audition for a role in a video for Jamaican-American hip-hop artist Will.I.Am's next single.

Also in December, Cheryl revealed that notwithstanding all the success with the band, marriage was the best thing she'd experienced so far. She told the *News of the World*: 'I still get butterflies when I'm going to see Ashley or when he calls me. We both work away a lot, so time together is precious. We make an effort to go out on dates, but I find it difficult to glam up for him as I always look that way for work. Weirdly, Ashley loves it when I don't wear a scrap of make-up and I'm in my tracksuit. He tells me I look gorgeous and I say: "Are you having a laugh?"'

She also admitted that Ashley had shattered all the preconceptions she had had regarding footballers. 'I had a stereotypical image of a footballer in my head before we met, but he was nothing like that. I was surprised when he always rang on time, or turned up to a date five minutes early with a bunch of flowers. I believe he's my reward for all the shit I've had in the past.'

But on 8 December 2007, Cheryl's life would be thrown into turmoil when Ashley dropped a bombshell that would leave her utterly destroyed.

Chapter 23
LIFE GETS COLD

Cheryl Cole was feeling a little snuffly when she arrived at Sketch bar and restaurant in London to watch her bandmate Nicola Roberts' fashion show on 18 January 2008.

For the past few weeks, Cheryl hadn't been able to shift a nagging cold that had taken hold over the Christmas period, and today's damp drizzly weather wasn't exactly helping. The last thing she needed to do in her poorly state was to trek across London and get photographed in the rain. But she knew she had no choice in the matter: there was no way she could let Nicola down by not showing up. So, reluctantly, she braced the horrors of the morning, hopped into a people carrier with Kimberley and headed into central London. When she arrived at the venue, the paparazzi appeared to be particularly fierce, surrounding the girls as they tried to make their way inside. Cheryl, having finally escaped the crush, joined Nicola in the main hall, where she was busy rehearsing the fashion show.

The whole event was the exciting culmination of Nicola's episode of *The Passions of Girls Aloud*. Her task was to design and produce a make-up range specifically for pale skin. She said she was fed up with hiding behind a fake tan all these years and was ready to embrace her own natural colour.

After the catwalk show, which went down a storm, the girls mingled backstage and posed for photographs for an *OK!* exclusive, answering questions about their day, and Cheryl explained how she hadn't really enjoyed her festive period all that much. 'I had a terrible Christmas,' she said. 'It was really awful. I had this cold all the way through, so it wasn't a lot of fun.' However, she seemed brighter now and even let slip that she was hoping to start a family with Ashley after the upcoming tour came to an end.

But those eagerly anticipated plans were dramatically put on hold just seven days later, when Cheryl's life was turned upside down. The *Sun* had contacted Cheryl's PR to let her camp know that a story was going to break that Ashley had allegedly cheated on her with a hairdresser. The couple had had to endure girls' accusations that they'd slept with Ashley before and each time they had been proven as liars.

Normally, Cheryl would have shrugged off the claim as yet another attempt by a kiss-and-tell girl to make some money out of a famous footballer. She trusted Ashley. She had said time and time again that she never had any reason to doubt him and was convinced he had been true to her.

'It doesn't bother me when I see pictures of him coming out of clubs with girls trying to throw themselves on him because I know he's not interested in them,' she once said in the *Mirror*. 'We actually have a good laugh over some of the stuff people write. When you start believing stories over your man, there are problems with the relationship anyway. I would always take Ashley's word over anyone unless I had solid, hard evidence something was definitely true. It just hasn't been an issue and it won't become one – we trust each other.'

But this time was different. Cheryl knew that this particular claim had legs. In fact, she had been expecting this story to come out eventually. She recalled in the *News of the World* how several weeks previously, on 8 December, Ashley had arrived home in the morning, after a big night out, looking terrible. His face was dazed and his clothes were covered in vomit. Of course, Cheryl knew immediately that something was up. Before she could say a thing, however, he hugged her tightly, broke down in tears and told her that something terrible had happened . . .

The night before, he and some mates had met up to enjoy a few drinks and stopped off at the CC Club in central London. While they were there, they were joined by a group of girls, one of whom was a hairdresser called Aimee Walton, who got chatting to them. As Premiership footballers, they were used to the attention of girls, but these ones seemed fun and nice enough – so together they downed vodka cocktail after vodka cocktail.

As the evening progressed, and Ashley became more and more tipsy, one of the party suggested they go back to their flat at Princess Park Manor to watch boxer Ricky Hatton's world title fight on their big-screen TV. The girls, no doubt unable to believe they were hanging out with some of Britain's top sports stars, readily accepted the invitation and headed back with them.

But it wasn't an easy ride. While two of Ashley's mates

jumped in a cab, he and another friend, CJ, got a lift with the girls in their car. As they wound their way through the streets of London heading north, Ashley, who by now was totally out of it, complained that he wasn't feeling well, and before the girls could pull over he ended up throwing up all over himself. When they arrived back at the flat, Ashley, barely able to walk, had to be helped inside and Aimee insisted that she would take care of him. Putting him to bed, she headed to the kitchen to fetch a bucket and to get some damp cloths to clean up the mess. What happened after that Ashley claimed not to remember.

However, in her own story for the *Sun*, Aimee alleged that the pair of them had had sex several times. She also revealed that during one bout of passion, Ashley had actually vomited, before mouthwashing and carrying on.

Although Cheryl was prepared for the story, it was still a blow. How could he have done this to her? Okay, so she trusted him when he told her he couldn't remember doing anything with this Aimee girl, but he had put himself into a situation in which he could be taken advantage of. And could she really believe that Ashley had not done anything? Was his memory loss just a convenient way of avoiding the truth?

She'd always said that if Ashley cheated on her, she would just leave, knowing there was no future. But now she was faced with the possibility that the worst had happened, what would she do? She still loved Ashley as much as she did before he'd come clean and even though he had hurt her, she couldn't bring herself to love him any less. But then she was angry at him, furious that he could do that to her, could make her feel this way.

He knew that she was a loyal wife who would never do anything to hurt him and that she expected the same from her man. And now he appeared to have thrown it all away. Cheryl revealed in her *News of the World* interview how she told Ashley she didn't want him near her that day and told him that he had to sleep in the spare bedroom. For the next few days, tensions in the household were fraught. She still couldn't forgive him for what he was alleged to have done. She was feeling hurt and she couldn't bring herself to look at him. They started to row constantly. Joan, who was living with them at the time, knew something was up and asked Cheryl if there was a problem. Not one to keep secrets from her mum, she eventually broke down and told her mum what had happened.

As days passed, Cheryl began to soften. As Ashley had football commitments and Cheryl had planned to head back to Newcastle to be with her family, the couple spent Christmas apart. But during this time, Cheryl came to realize that she simply couldn't give up on her Ashley. He was the man she had married and had promised to stick with through good times and bad. With a new year just a few days away, she wanted to kick off 2008 on a positive track and even began to think about finally starting that family she had spoken about so often.

But then Aimee's kiss-and-tell in the *Sun* in the new year brought all the memories back, only this time, Aimee had elaborated on what Ashley had told her. If Aimee's story was to be believed then Ashley had definitely cheated on Cheryl. He had slept with another woman behind her back. Nevertheless, in public Cheryl stood by Ashley and spoke to the *News of the World* two days later to tell the nation that she believed her husband hadn't slept with Aimee. And how did she know this? Because, Cheryl countered, if he were as drunk as Aimee said he was, he wouldn't have been able to perform. 'I know Ashley intimately,' Cheryl said. 'When he's under the influence he *isn't* capable. When I heard what this girl had said I realized she'd made part of the story up. And, to be honest, that has helped me get through this.'

She went on to say that when she had read Aimee's allegation she felt like she'd been punched. 'Obviously I felt sick to the stomach. What woman and wife wouldn't? And to be honest I felt humiliated and crushed that this girl was saying these things and people were believing it. I only told my mum. I adore the girls from the band but I hadn't even told them. It was something that Ashley and I had to get through together.'

She explained why she was planning to stick with Ashley: 'We love each other, I adore Ashley and we spent time talking about things. I'm still hurt and angry but we've been working things through since December and we're now hoping to move forward and rebuild our relationship . . .'

Unfortunately, things got worse. On the same day the *News of the World* hit the stands, rival newspapers ran more kiss-and-tells from glamour girls Brooke Healy and Coralie Robinson, who claimed they too had slept with Ashley and had been paid off by his agent. Worse still, it was then alleged that Ashley's agent had given Aimee money for an abortion when she thought she might be pregnant following their encounter.

These new developments drove Cheryl crazy. Now she really didn't know what to think. Were these girls just opportunists, cashing in on his current notoriety? Or had Ashley been fooling around behind her back all this time? Could she believe her husband anymore?

She was devastated. How could he have done this to her? How could he have put her through this? What could she believe anymore? Could she just forgive and forget? She'd always said she would leave him if he cheated, but was she strong enough to do it now?

Cheryl tried to deal with it in the best way she could by throwing herself into her work. She joined the girls at a location in London to shoot the promo for 'Can't Speak French'. The shoot was a sombre affair with the crew tiptoeing around Cheryl, who hardly said a word all day and kept herself to herself. The rest of the girls would take turns to sit with her, and make sure she was all right and give her warm, reassuring hugs. Sometimes, she'd dash off set and sob alone. It was clear that it was all beginning to get to her.

After the shoot wrapped, Cheryl made a decision. She needed some time alone. She couldn't be around Ashley right now. She needed some time to think. He had risked destroying their marriage and the last thing she wanted to do was to see him. So on the advice of her management, she decided that the best thing to do was not only to move out of their Oxshott mansion, but to get out of the country and away from it all, so she could have some space to think about what to do next.

Of course, she didn't want to go away on her own, so she asked Nicola and Kimberley to join her on a break in Thailand. That was far enough away from the UK for them to avoid seeing any more lurid headlines. When they got there, the girls booked themselves into a £2,000-a-night villa. It was reported by the *Sun* that a holidaymaker supposedly overhead Cheryl saying that she thought Ashley was 'damaged goods' and that she knew something was wrong when she confronted him about some woman and he made up some excuse rather than denying it outright.

The stress of the situation was getting to her but her bandmates helped her get through it. Later, Nicola Roberts would tell *OK!* magazine about their time in Thailand. 'We had an amazing time, it was so relaxing. We had such a laugh . . . When we were there, we ordered loads of cheesecakes. And then when they came we were so full up from our main meal, we couldn't eat them.'

After Thailand, Cheryl and the girls headed to LA, where Cheryl was set to film the second half of her documentary for *Passions*. Her challenge was to become a street dancer, and this time round she would be auditioning for a spot in the video for Will.I.Am's aptly titled single 'Heartbreaker'.

When they arrived at LAX airport the girls were horrified to discover that their car hadn't turned up and they found themselves surrounded by up to fifty paparazzi snapping at them. Some foolhardy shutterbugs threw questions at Cheryl such as, 'Have you forgiven Ashley?', to which she'd cut them dead with a 'You're hilarious, you are. You should be a comedian' or 'Do you have a wife? No, I don't suppose you do looking like that!' But, like a trouper, she muddled through, even stopping to pose with a little child for a photograph.

The paps clung to her like leeches for the duration of her stay there, chasing her down Sunset Strip one minute, following her to the Villa nightclub the next, where the girls partied the night away. 'LA was wild, and the three of us had a brilliant time out there,' Nicola said. 'We hadn't been out like that for a long time and it was really good. But there were so many paparazzi there that it didn't feel like a holiday.'

The girls about town even attracted the attention of some fellow celebrities during their stay in LA. When they spent an evening at the trendy Mondrian Hotel, they were chatted up by US TV star Will Luke and his pal Kenny Rufus, who were filming their own reality show called *Parking Lot Pimps*. According to Will, he and Kenny saw Cheryl standing by the reception desk sobbing.

'She was inconsolable and looked so sad I had to see if she was OK,' he told the *News of the World*. 'We found out she and her friends were in some band called Girls Aloud but none of us had ever heard of them. We just thought they were very cute girls who were very drunk. We all got chatting and when Nicola asked if we wanted to go up to Cheryl's room I just looked at Kenny and said, "Let's roll with it."'

Cheryl and her hairdresser, Lisa Laudat, supposedly went upstairs first and Will, Kenny and their camera crew followed with Nicola and Kimberley. When they got to the room, Lisa opened the door and, behind her, Will could see Cheryl sitting on the bed crying. He quoted Psalm 30 Verse 5 from the Bible: 'Weeping may endure for the night but joy comes in the morning.'

Will told the *News of the World* that Lisa checked with Cheryl if it was okay to let the boys in. She wiped her tears and agreed. Inside, Will asked Cheryl what was wrong and Lisa explained what had happened back home in the UK. Will tried to reassure Cheryl that everything would be all right and encouraged her to have a good time. He even tried to get her to join him at church the next day.

'I was trying to get her to smile and it seemed to work,' Will explained. As the night progressed, Cheryl appeared to relax and occasionally threw her arms around Will and told him and Kenny, 'When you come [to England] you better tell us you're there because we can show you a good night out.'

Will said Cheryl kept telling him, 'You make me feel so good. You made me feel much better,' and she told him she loved his bald head and kissed it twice. He said he felt like the luckiest man alive. The party ended around 4 a.m. when Lisa told the boys that the girls needed to get some sleep.

Once Cheryl had finished filming her scenes for *The Passions of Girls Aloud*, and, thanks to that show, having danced in the video to Will.I.Am's single 'Heartbreaker', she and the girls flew back to London to attend the 2008 BRIT Awards at Earls Court arena on 20 February. It would be her first public appearance since the news had broken about Ashley's alleged infidelity.

But before she hit the red carpet, it was reported that Cheryl met with Ashley for a showdown in her hotel room at the Royal Gardens Hotel in Kensington, West London. According to the *Daily Mail* their hour-long meeting was tense and Cheryl found it hard to look Ashley in the eye without dissolving into tears. But even though Ashley had pleaded for forgiveness, Cheryl knew she wasn't ready to wipe the slate clean just yet. She was still hurting inside and there was no way she could just forgive and forget. There was still a lot of work Ashley would have to do if he wanted to win back her heart and, more importantly, her trust.

That evening, Cheryl arrived at the BRITs with bandmates Sarah Harding, Nicola Roberts and Kimberley Walsh. Only Nadine Coyle was a no-show, as she'd missed her flight from LA after discovering she'd mislaid her passport, fuelling yet more conspiracy theories that she was about to quit the band.

As she posed for pictures on the red carpet at the BRITs, Cheryl dazzled in a canary-yellow mini-dress and looked strong and determined, showing no signs of the heartache she was suffering inside. After the show, she headed off to the Universal party with the girls for a few drinks but left shortly afterwards, preferring to spend some time alone with her thoughts.

Soon after, strong rumours emerged that Cheryl had taken Ashley back, though nothing was officially confirmed. As the nation continued to lap up the rumours, Cheryl's friends rallied round her and offered their sympathy. Pop singer Jamelia, who had been a guest at Cheryl and Ashley's wedding, said she knew what Cheryl was going through. 'It's devastating for them,' she told *Fabulous* magazine, 'and I feel for her because I've been through that hell. There is a sleazy, seedy side to the football industry that's hard to deal with. I just hope Cheryl gets through it okay.'

When rumours reached the tabloids that Cheryl had in fact taken Ashley back, Lizzie Cundy, wife of Chelsea footballer Jason, and friend of the Coles, was thrilled with their decision. She told *OK!* magazine: 'I couldn't be happier. Ashley has admitted what he got up to, and I bet there's no one in the world who feels worse than him right now. He's been a silly boy and he knows it! I wouldn't be surprised now if they start that family they have wanted for so long.'

Lizzie also said that she thought all marriages have ups and downs and that Cheryl and Ashley shouldn't let Aimee Walton ruin their relationship, as it was so clear that Ashley loved Cheryl. Lizzie, who is friends with many of the WAGs, also theorized about why she thought so many footballers ended up falling foul of their wives, saying: 'The main problem these days is that these young footballers earn so much, they think they can get away with anything. And it doesn't help that these girls target footballers and sell these stories and ruin lives and break up relationships.'

There was a positive to be found in all of this, however, as it seemed that applying herself to her singing through these hard times was really paying off for Cheryl. In March 2008, it emerged that, during her time in LA in February, Cheryl had not only appeared in the video for Will.I.Am's 'Heartbreaker', she had also been invited to re-record the track with Will.I.Am, featuring her on backing vocals.

When she appeared on *The Graham Norton Show* with Will.I.Am, she gave an excellent and convincing performance. Will.I.Am reckoned that the song was a good way for Cheryl to exorcize some of her anger, and was quoted in the *Daily Star* as saying: 'On the record she's calling me a heartbreaker and she says "effing jerk". Every time she says that she's really letting off some anger. When Cheryl came to LA she said: "I love this song, I'm going through a lot right now, I could really relate to this."'

A little while later, Cheryl and the girls were back at work, shooting a commercial for new chocolate bar KitKat Senses. The ad was shot on one of the coldest nights of the year on the steps of University College, London, and the poor girls were forced to wear the flimsiest dresses they'd had to wear in a long time. But, having been paid a six-figure sum for the campaign, they managed to pull through.

For the interviews that tied in with the campaign in March, Cheryl's management team laid down some ground rules to all publications that their journalists were not permitted to ask anything about Ashley or what had been happening over the past few months. If they broke the rules, then the interview was over. But that didn't mean the public weren't given an insight into how life was for Cheryl at that time. In an interview with the *Mirror* newspaper, Cheryl admitted that her four bandmates were helping her to survive.

'I often think to myself, if I'm having a sad moment or an angry moment, if I didn't have these four in my life it would be worthless. Everyone's here to help each other. We stabilize each other. Whatever any of us is going through, bad or good, we have each other.'

In the same interview, Kimberley spoke about the special relationship she shared with the girls. 'We've been together so much we're like sisters – and you know what you're like about your sisters. We're very protective of each other. We can say stuff about each other, but no one else can.'

Cheryl also showed signs that she was on the road to recovery and joked on Newcastle's Metro Radio station that she had the hots for Ashley's former boss, ex-Chelsea manager José Mourinho. 'He's cool. I fancy him because he's dead cocky and arrogant. I've only ever seen him from a distance though. It's a secret crush . . . maybe not any more!' She also let slip that her baby plans were back in her mind again. 'I've been broody since I was about sixteen. I'd love to have a big family.'

When the band kicked off their *Tangled Up* UK tour in Belfast in May, Cheryl dedicated the band's track 'I'll Stand By You' to 'anyone who is going through a hard time at the moment'. The audience gave her an extremely warm reception.

While Ashley and Cheryl still hadn't been seen in public together, word got around that things were slowly getting back to rights between the two. When the girls reached Birmingham, Ashley turned up backstage with Cheryl's mum Joan. Speaking to *Hello!* magazine, Cheryl revealed that

Ashley had sent her some flowers and a bunch of balloons, but had spoilt the surprise by sending her a text beforehand to ask her if the flowers had arrived. 'He blew the surprise,' she said, warmly. 'He didn't really think that through, did he? Still, they are really beautiful.'

It would only be a matter of time before the nation would know for sure that Cheryl and Ashley's marriage was back on track. And it wasn't just her personal life that was looking brighter: Cheryl was about to be offered an opportunity that would change her life and take her back to where her journey with Girls Aloud had begun. Only this time, *she* would be calling the shots.

Chapter 24
CHERYL GETS THE X FACTOR

As she swept past the waiting paparazzi, Cheryl was facing one of the toughest days of her career: she was going to have to make hard decisions that could make or break the dreams of thousands of hopefuls.

Would she be able to cope with youngsters breaking down in tears in front of her? She knew she had to be strong and consider each and every person on their merits: she owed it to them and to her fellow judges to be fair and honest no matter what.

Of course, having been through the process herself, Cheryl knew that whatever comments she made, she had to be sensitive. She wasn't one of those people who would purposefully crush someone's dreams: she of all people knew how important it was to dream. But she also knew that it was important to let people know if they were wasting their time. It was best to let them down gently, so they could go off and find another path to take.

It was a strange feeling for Cheryl to think that she'd come full circle. Just six years ago, she had been one of those nervous auditionees standing in a queue waiting to be judged. And from what she could remember it was the most arduous experience of her life.

'I sang almost every note out of tune,' Cheryl told Holly Willoughby on ITV2's *The Xtra Factor*. 'Nerves can totally change your voice and I don't think I was that good. I can't believe I made it through.'

But now she was sitting on the *X Factor* judging panel, deciding how someone's life would pan out. The show's creator, Simon Cowell, proved a huge supporter of Cheryl's appointment, perhaps surprisingly, given his criticisms of Girls Aloud back in 2003. Not long after the girls had enjoyed their first number-one single with 'Sound Of The Underground', Simon took it upon himself to poke fun at his rival Louis Walsh's latest signing, focusing particularly on Cheryl Tweedy. The *Sun* reported him as saying: 'The Geordie girl, she's crap, I remember seeing her last audition and she couldn't sing a note in tune. I'm amazed she got through.'

Luckily, Cheryl forgave Simon's typically outrageous comments, and although she had turned down his offer to appear as a judge on *Britain's Got Talent* in 2007, she declared at the time, 'I think he has a good heart. He really is a big pussy cat.' Cowell wasn't dissuaded by her rejection of his offer, and his persistence paid off when she agreed to appear alongside him on *The X Factor*. However, when he was later grilled by Cheryl on the show about his 2003 comments, he denied any memory of having made them!

Simon explained his determination to get Cheryl on board

at *The X Factor* conference: 'I have always wanted Cheryl to be part of one of these programmes. I was first impressed by her when she was taking part in *Celebrity Apprentice* and she came to me and charmed me out of a very big cheque.'

But Simon wasn't the only issue. A few years previously, Dannii Minogue, Cheryl's fellow judge on *The X Factor*, had been involved in a couple of run-ins with Cheryl and Girls Aloud. When Cheryl was asked by *Top of the Pops* magazine in 2003 whether she would consider plastic surgery, Cheryl stated that 'if you're not happy within yourself and you've got the money to have plastic surgery, then go for it', but added that she felt some stars went too far – and cited Dannii Minogue. 'I think Dannii Minogue should get all her plastic surgery reduced and go back to the way she was before. She doesn't look natural. I don't think men find that attractive.'

Dannii later had her say at a 2003 summer roadshow gig that both she and Girls Aloud were attending, though her comments were directed at Nicola. 'I think the redhead's got it in for me,' she said in the *Mirror*. 'After a show in Scotland, Nicola was saying vile stuff about me. I saw her at last year's Disney Awards and just smiled. I mean, the punch-ups, going to court . . . I don't want to get involved – I'm no chav!'

However, it seemed as though both Dannii and Cheryl had laid the past to rest, with Dannii congratulating her on landing the new job back in June 2008 at a press conference for the show. In an interview for *OK!* magazine around the time of the start of *The X Factor*, Dannii said that she wasn't sure if everything Cheryl had supposedly said about her was true or if she had merely been misquoted. Besides, Dannii was probably relieved that there was some new blood on the programme. Her experience on the show the previous year hadn't exactly been the most pleasurable. 'I was just very unwelcome,' Dannii told *OK!* 'Louis and Sharon said that I shouldn't have been there: "She's not got the music backing." That was tough to hear and it upset me. But hearing them say that made me more determined. When someone says I don't have the qualifications to do something then I will prove that I do.'

But while Cheryl's appointment proved a popular choice with viewers, Cheryl's pals the Sugababes didn't seem as convinced. Keisha Buchanan told Virgin Radio: 'Actually, I would have preferred Boy George. He has got so much more experience, and so many more years behind him. I think he would have been much better as the judge.' Amelle Berrabah agreed: 'Yeah, Boy George has generations more on her. Not that Cheryl hasn't got any experience, but someone who has been going for as long as he has should have been given a chance.' But Heidi Range rated Cheryl's chances on the show. 'Well, Cheryl did come from reality TV herself . . . so I guess that does make sense. But she could do with some more experience.'

Sweeping into Arsenal's Emirates Stadium in London, Cheryl shrugged off any thoughts of these negative comments when she was warmly greeted by the *X Factor* production team, who talked her through the day's events. Afterwards, she joined the judges. Dannii leaned in and wished her luck. 'I know how scary it is,' she told her, 'but just be yourself, that's why you're here, that's why we're all chosen, to just be ourselves.'

And then, at last, the moment arrived. It was time to become one of the four judges on *The X Factor*. Cheryl told an ITV press conference that she felt nervous on her first day, taking her seat at the judges' table. Simon, Louis and Dannii had years of judging experience between them; she was the newbie. Would she be able to cope with the pressures of making or breaking hopefuls' dreams?

The first contestant up was nineteen-year-old Dominic Moone, who unnerved her straight away. Even before he sang a note, he broke down in tears before them, overcome by the moment. But he managed to pull himself together after a quick breather. Unfortunately, his performance just didn't cut it and Cheryl had to agree with her fellow judges that it was a 'no'.

Once she knew she could cope with a situation like young Dominic, over the next few days Cheryl got into the swing of things. As the show visited Cardiff, Manchester, Birmingham and Glasgow, Cheryl became more comfortable in her role and actually started to enjoy her time on the panel, even joking with contestants that they wouldn't want Louis as their boss because 'he's rubbish'. She was firm and gave the contestants her honest opinions.

Of course, breaking someone's heart wasn't easy for Cheryl and tears flowed freely, and one contestant in particular proved to be too hard for Cheryl to judge. When the show arrived in Manchester, a twenty-four-year-old wannabe called Nikk Mager managed to turn Cheryl into a sobbing wreck. When he strode into the audition room, she looked up to see the same Nikk Mager with whom she had auditioned on *Popstars: The Rivals* six years previously.

Although Nikk hadn't made it through to One True Voice, he had gone on to enjoy a brief pop career with the runner-up band, Phixx. Since then, however, he had been playing working men's clubs, but still wanted to make it big. So when he heard about the new series of *The X Factor* he decided he'd give his singing another shot. Cheryl was shocked to see him: it had been years since they'd seen each other. She knew that this was going to be a hard audition to sit through, so she turned to Simon and said, 'Look, I can't do this one, it wouldn't be fair.' Simon reassured her that it would be okay and told her to sit through the audition.

When Nikk began to sing Bette Midler's 'The Rose', it was clear on the faces of Louis, Dannii and Simon that the audition wasn't going well and Cheryl became very uncomfortable. She knew that Nikk had talent, she had seen that six years ago, but she also knew that the other judges weren't responding well to his audition. There was no way she could destroy what he had himself called his last chance at success. As Simon told Nikk that his journey was over, Cheryl couldn't take any more, and said, 'I can't do this,' then stepped down from the panel while the judges gave Nikk their review.

Standing in the wings, Cheryl could see Nikk's face fall as Simon, Dannii and Louis gave him the bad news that he wasn't going to make it through to boot camp. Cheryl really had been one of the lucky ones. Six years ago she had appeared on a TV show and now because of that she was in Girls Aloud, one of the most successful female bands of all time. Meanwhile, hopefuls like Nikk Mager were cast to the wayside every day.

When the judges had finished giving Nikk their decision, Cheryl dashed over to him and held him close, telling him she was sorry that it had worked out the way it had. Afterwards, he told the *Huddersfield Gazette*: 'I was gutted, absolutely devastated. For a full week it was like my world had ended. I felt cheated because I believe I should have gone through. I thought it had gone okay. It could have gone better – I had had one hour's sleep and had a chest infection so I wasn't at my best. But in my opinion I showed potential and should have gone through to the next stage. After I had finished, Cheryl came over and looked really upset and after I left she apparently started crying. It's nice to know that she still cares and didn't want to see me go through that.'

After his audition, Cheryl had indeed broken down in tears, and admitted that she now realized that her job on *The X Factor* was going to be harder than even she had thought. 'That was awful,' she sobbed on the show. 'You see someone like Nikk struggle for years, just to be crushed again. I can't imagine how he's feeling.'

But she had to force herself to deal with the cruel side of her job, and took comfort from the fact that she was finding some rich new talent: for every one hundred or so contestants they rejected, the judges would stumble across a rare find, like Alexandra, the sixteen-year-old from Bridgend who dazzled them with her stunning rendition of 'Fields Of Gold', or Austin Drage who sang Boyz II Men's 'End Of The Road', or boyband JLS, whose tight harmonies during their version of Shai's 'If I Ever Fall In Love' impressed Cheryl so much she declared she wanted them in her category when the show moved on to the stage where each judge individually mentored a group. And then there'd be wannabes like Rachel Hylton, who at twenty-six was the mother of five children, the oldest of whom was thirteen. When she stood before them she moved them with her dedication to better her life, after years of drug addiction and imprisonment. And when she sang Amy Winehouse's 'I'm No Good', the judges were blown away, not just because she had an amazing voice but because she had real passion and a hunger to succeed.

Cheryl would later reveal that her experience during the auditions had been tough and that every night she would go home physically and emotionally exhausted. 'At the end of every day I would go home and cry,' she told *The People*. 'It's such a rollercoaster. By the end you are mentally drained. The only way I can deal with it is to go home and talk it through with my mum.'

As the audition process rolled on, Cheryl was able to fit in some personal time with Ashley, during which they had managed to put the past behind them once and for all. During the Manchester auditions in June, Ashley joined Cheryl at the Radisson Hotel for her twenty-fifth birthday celebrations. According to *Hello!* magazine the couple spent the late afternoon holed up in their room before heading out to Wings, a local Chinese restaurant, where she was joined by her mum Joan, Ashley's mum Sue, her manager Hillary Shaw and a small gaggle of friends and family – including Nicola Roberts. Just prior to her birthday Cheryl had commented to *Hello!* magazine that she was nervous about turning twenty-five. 'I was only eighteen when I joined the group. But twenty-five! I feel so old.' By the time the champagne started to flow, however, she forgot all about reaching such a milestone age.

Inside the restaurant, Ashley had arranged for balloons to be set up around their table, and when the moment arrived for the birthday cake to be brought through, the group sang a rousing rendition of 'Happy Birthday'. 'It was quite a simple

celebration, but perfect,' one of the guests confided to *Hello!*
'Cheryl was thrilled with all her gifts, which included an
Yves Saint Laurent clutch bag from Nicola, a beautiful gold
chain from Hillary and some scented candles from Dannii
Minogue.' But Cheryl's favourite gifts came from husband
Ashley, who had thought long and hard about what to get
his wife. Among his booty of gifts was a Hublot Big Bang
Cappuccino watch, worth an estimated £35,000, a £525 pair
of high-heeled black shoe boots by exclusive designer Rupert
Sanderson, and several sets of Agent Provocateur lingerie,
once again suggesting that the fire and spice was back in their
relationship! 'He picked out all the presents himself,' the same
guest revealed to *Hello!* 'Cheryl didn't have a clue what she
was getting. He got it just right. She loved them all – what girl
wouldn't?'

So it seemed that after much pleading, Ashley had finally
convinced Cheryl to take him back. As Ashley had launched
a legal case against the newspapers regarding the allegations
back in January, neither Ashley nor Cheryl were able to talk
publicly about their relationship, but they managed to let
everyone know that things were better by being photographed
on a trip to Spain. The couple were seen strolling hand in hand
across a beach, and frolicking in a pool. While her wedding
ring was still missing from Cheryl's finger, it looked very much
like the relationship was going well.

Cheryl still managed to have a spot of harmless fun on *The
X Factor*, when a good-looking lad called Joseph Chukukere
walked in for his audition. As he launched into a soulful
version of 'Ain't No Sunshine', Cheryl couldn't stop herself from
smiling, and when he reached the end of his audition Dannii

joked, 'I think you have a "yes" from Cheryl already.' Cheryl didn't deny it, exclaiming, 'Oh my God, you are gorgeous!' When he left the room she playfully sighed, 'He was cute.' The press, of course, made a mountain out of a molehill, and the *Mirror* quoted Joseph's girlfriend as saying, 'Cheryl can keep her hands to herself.' But the girl needn't have bothered. Cheryl was delighted to be reunited with Ashley, and by September the wedding rings were back on again.

And it seemed that Cheryl was universally popular in her role on *The X Factor*. Well, almost. Charlotte Church said on her Channel 4 show that Cheryl's refusal to judge Nikk Mager proved she 'had no backbone'. Cheryl's *X Factor* colleague, presenter Dermot O'Leary, however, was swift to defend her at a press conference – saying that in many ways Cheryl was similar to her predecessor, the well-loved Sharon Osbourne. 'Odd as it sounds, in many ways Cheryl is almost a like-for-like replacement. Sharon has that same maternal instinct and she's an incredibly ballsy lady. Cheryl brings all that. She exudes an incredible warmth because she has been there, done that.'

If any proof was needed of Cheryl's popularity, it came when *Heat* magazine declared her Britain's Top Style Icon, with her beating off the likes of Victoria Beckham, Coleen Rooney and ITV2's *Xtra Factor* presenter Holly Willoughby. Laughing about the accolade, Cheryl told *Heat* magazine: 'Women think that men think you look best dolled up – but as a band Girls Aloud are always so dressed up, so I'm preferred in my trackie with my hair up and no make-up . . . When I've got no make-up on, hair scraped off my head, [Ashley] always says, "Oh, you look cute!"'

The year may have begun with a bump, but overall 2008 was turning out to be brilliant for Cheryl. Girls Aloud had sold out arenas, she had landed a job on *The X Factor* and she was as in love with Ashley as she had been at the start of their relationship. She had come so far: no longer was she the little girl from Heaton with stars in her eyes. Now she was a successful woman, and although she had suffered some hardships, she had pulled through gallantly.

All in all, Cheryl had now reached a point in her life where she was content, although there was still lots more for the ambitious lass to achieve. And with her man by her side once more, it seemed she had the confidence to try anything. The coming autumn would see Girls Aloud's fifth studio album released, and the girls' careers appeared set to continue to dazzle.

But music, by now, was second nature to Cheryl. It was the challenge of her new TV career as a talent-show judge that was capturing her – and the nation's – imagination. But she hardly dared dream for what she truly wished for: to come out on top at the end of the series, having made someone else's ambition a reality. Surely that was too much to hope for?

Chapter 25
THE X FACTOR GETS TOUGH

As Cheryl's first series of *The X Factor* progressed, rumours emerged once again that relations between Cheryl and her fellow judge Dannii Minogue had become strained. According to various reports, Dannii was unhappy that she seemed to have been sidelined in the final edits of the show, the ones that were eventually broadcast.

Publicly, Dannii said that she understood that, as the new judge, Cheryl had to appear more on screen to establish her with the audience. However, rival panellist Louis Walsh, who was never short of a soundbite, said that he believed Simon Cowell had forgotten about Dannii this time round. 'He definitely flirted with Dannii throughout last year's series, but he seems to have moved on,' he told *Heat* magazine. 'He's flirting with Cheryl this year.'

When asked if he thought Simon had turned his attention to a 'more attractive' model, Louis responded: 'Yes, you might say that. He's definitely paying attention to Cheryl now, not Dannii.'

But rivalries were soon forgotten as Cheryl and the other judges continued to see more talented – and not-so-talented – wannabes pass through the audition room. One, called Dav John, turned up announcing he was to sing 'What Comes Around' by Justin Timberlake. Sadly, his mumbling performance fell short of anything his idol could have achieved. As Simon and Louis dissolved into hysterics beside her, Cheryl found it hard to keep a straight face. After the audition, she kindly said, 'You look like Justin,' albeit with the closing statement, 'but you sound nothing like him.'

Yet if she thought Dav John was a funny fish, Cheryl wasn't prepared for one particular set of auditionees: two brothers from Wales, who called themselves Ant and Seb. Before they entered the audition room, they told Dermot O'Leary that they were confident that their unique brand of pop could give Wales its first win on the show.

'*The X Factor* has never had anyone like us on before,' Sebastian boasted. And he was right. As they walked into the room, the judges could tell instantly that these boys would be TV gold. When asked who they compared themselves to, Sebastian likened their duo to Usher and P. Diddy, with a mix of Rick Astley.

The hapless pair failed to see the amusement on the judges' faces as they launched into their audition song, 'Mysterious Girl' by Peter Andre. It wasn't that Anton's voice was bad – he did actually sing in tune – it was Sebastian's MC interjections, encouraging the judges to 'C'mon, move your body', which hit a bum note. His badly timed, poorly executed rap caused the judges no end of mirth. Poor Cheryl, who tried desperately to keep her giggles in check, couldn't hold back her sniggers in the end, as the oddball pair continued to destroy the Peter Andre classic.

Needless to say, the brothers failed to make it through to boot camp. But many other hopefuls did manage to impress the tough foursome with some powerhouse vocals. Among the stand-out stars was sixteen-year-old Eoghan Quigg from Northern Ireland, who sang 'Tears In Heaven' by Eric Clapton and 'Home' by Michael Bublé. Widower Daniel Evans pulled at the heartstrings with his painfully sincere rendition of 'Sometimes When We Touch', while seventeen-year-old wannabe Diana Vickers, from Blackburn – who became immediately recognizable to viewers, with her kooky backcombed hair and a Dolores O'Riordan-style voice – stunned the judges with an emotional version of Damien Rice's 'The Blower's Daughter'.

Amy Winehouse-soundalike Laura White also wowed the panel – with a show-stopping cover of 'Somebody Else's Guy' – as did Alexandra Burke, a contestant from London who had made it through to the judges' houses part of the show three years before. Back then, Louis had shattered her dreams, telling her she hadn't made it through because he felt as though something was missing. Standing in front of the panel, the nineteen-year-old told them she had learned a lot since her last appearance on the programme – and then launched into an incredible version of 'Saving All My Love For You' by Whitney Houston.

As she reached the end of the first chorus, Simon raised his hand to stop her, and then asked Louis what he thought about her performance. It was good news for Alex: it appeared that the years had softened Louis's heart and he declared that she was excellent. Indeed, this time around, the judges were unanimous in revelling in the glory of the singer's vocals. Yet it was Cheryl who was moved the most. Unable to speak for tears, the normally tough little cookie uttered through sobs: 'I was blown away. I think you're amazing. I have goosebumps.'

When it came to deciding whether Alexandra deserved to go through to the next round, a humbled Cheryl said defiantly, 'It's not even a question. It's a one-hundred-per-cent yes.' Afterwards, the perceptive judge reflected: 'She was mind-blowing. She has something special.'

When *The X Factor* entered its boot-camp stage, it became clear to all the judges that 'the girls' were by far the strongest category – and each of them was keen to land the group. Cheryl, in particular, was keeping her fingers crossed that the show's producers would give her the chance to mentor the girls in the final stages of the series, especially when she saw how much talent some of the contestants had.

Laura White continued to impress. When she sang 'The First Time Ever I Saw Your Face' during boot camp, the panel were united in their praise for her. 'You blew me away,' Cheryl said, and Laura was seen through to the next day.

Yet when the hopeful performed Amy Winehouse's 'Back To Black', just a day later, Cheryl had second thoughts, commenting: 'She sounded like Amy Winehouse … but when she has had a few drinks.'

Luckily, that rare moment of inconsistency on Laura's part didn't affect the judges' overall feelings for her, and Laura – along with Alexandra Burke, Diana Vickers, Annastasia Baker, Hannah Bradbeer and Amy Connelly – was chosen to go through to the next round: the judges' houses. These six, uber-talented contestants cemented the panel's initial feelings that the girls' category was the strongest and, as they had been when boot camp began, all the judges were keen to get their hands on the group. But Cheryl was the lucky one – leaving Simon with the boys, Louis with the groups and Dannii with the over-25s.

Cheryl flew her hopefuls to a villa in Cannes. She knew all too well how the starry-eyed wannabes were feeling at this precise moment. They were one step away from the final stage – the live TV shows – and it was her life-changing decision that would determine whether or not they would continue on their journey. It was a particularly tough scenario for Cheryl because she had been in this very situation herself. Yet she knew that she had to do it. This was her job: to select the three most talented performers in her group.

Fortunately, the producers had given her the opportunity to choose a guest judge for this part of the audition process, who would work alongside Cheryl to help her identify her final three. She chose her bandmate and closest friend Kimberley Walsh. Working together, they would decide which contestants deserved to proceed further in the competition.

Cheryl advised the eager hopefuls not to let nerves affect their performances, as far as they were able. Each had to sing solo one last time for her and Kimberley. This really was the make-or-break moment. The girls gave it their all, singing their songs from the heart. Once all six had performed, it was ultimately left up to Cheryl to determine which three would make it through.

The decision was an incredibly hard one for her. No sooner had the contestants hurried back to the villa to await their fate than the Geordie burst into tears. 'I have just realized the responsibility I've got,' she sobbed.

Cheryl knew exactly what the girls were going through. She'd been there herself, experienced this moment first hand: when the course of the rest of her life had been in the hands of another, and she couldn't do anything about it.

It was this element of the show that had put her off taking part in *The X Factor* in the first place. She would be giving three people the chance of their lives, while dashing the dreams of another three. In the end, she reasoned that it was all part of the game; that this was a competition seeking the best talent the country had to offer.

Although Cheryl had Kimberley to assist her in making the hard decisions, she was on her own when it came to telling three of the girls – face to face – that their journey was at an end. First to discover her destiny was Annastasia Baker. She had impressed over the weeks, but during her performance at the villa she had fallen apart with nerves: an issue that Cheryl was forced to consider in rejecting her. Hannah was devastated to learn that she too would be proceeding no further, while young Amy was inconsolable to be told that she wouldn't be making the live finals.

When Diana Vickers sat down with Cheryl, she wasn't sure what the outcome would be. Cheryl didn't keep her waiting for too long – and revealed that she was indeed one of her three finalists. Diana was over the moon.

Next up was Laura White. When she joined Cheryl to discover her fate, her soon-to-be mentor played a similar trick to the one that Geri Halliwell had played on *Popstars: The Rivals* all those years ago. 'You have such a specific sound,' Cheryl began, 'and I'm not sure if the public would be able to relate to that.'

As the words slipped out, Laura looked crestfallen. Was her

journey over? Not likely. For Cheryl then hastily added, 'You are in the final three.' Laura was through, and she was beside herself.

Yet more was still to come. Cheryl saved her wickedest trick for Alexandra Burke, the girl who had fallen at this same hurdle on *The X Factor* three years before. 'I can only take three people through to the finals,' Cheryl explained clearly, and then she looked Alexandra in the eye. 'I didn't want to be the person to do this to you again.'

Alex – sensing that her journey was over once again, and at the identical stage at which she'd lost out in 2005 – was overcome with grief. She began sobbing uncontrollably, 'No, not again.'

Seeing how upset she was becoming, Cheryl was no longer able to keep Alex in the dark and gladly announced, 'You're in the final three.' Overjoyed, a speechless Alex threw her arms around Cheryl's neck and together they tumbled back into the seat. Alex squeezed her mentor with all her might. She couldn't believe that, after three years, she had finally made it through to the live shows. Surely she was destined to make it as a star now – or so she hoped.

When the first week of studio shows arrived, in early October 2008, the memories came flooding back to Cheryl as she remembered the very first Saturday night that she had stepped out on to the *Popstars: The Rivals* stage. As she watched Dermot introduce each contestant, she was transported back to 2002, when she was just an eighteen-year-old wannabe, desperately hoping she would triumph on the show. She remembered the quaking heart, the butterflies in her stomach and the dry mouth all too well.

It had been a nerve-wracking, but ultimately fruitful experience for her. Not everyone was going to be a winner here, she knew that. But for the next few weeks, these talented people had the opportunity to shine and to convince viewers across the UK that they indeed had 'the X factor'. Cheryl was sure that she and the other judges had done well in selecting the cream of the crop – but she was also glad to be done with having the responsibility of make-or-break decisions on her shoulders. Now, it was down to the public.

As the weeks passed by, it was clear that Cheryl's girls were by far the most interesting acts: each demonstrated a unique sound, not often heard on shows like this. Diana was very folksy; Laura had a cutting-edge soul vibe; and Alexandra proved to have a belting R&B/pop vocal. Week after week, the girls delivered amazing performances. It seemed ever more likely that Cheryl might pull off an unprecedented coup and take her three contestants all the way to the prestigious final – much to the chagrin of the other judges.

But, just over a month into the run of live shows, during the Mariah Carey-themed week, Cheryl and her protégée Laura were in for a shock. After the phone lines had closed and the votes had been counted, it emerged that Laura, together with over-25s contestant Ruth Lorenzo, was in the bottom two. Cheryl was devastated. As early on as boot camp, she had been sure that Laura had what it took to reach the final. True, the judges' comments on that particular week's performance hadn't been great, but surely Laura deserved to continue on her journey?

Singing for what could be her last time on *The X Factor*, Laura chose 'Over The Rainbow' as her survival song, while Ruth belted out the rock version of 'Knocking On Heaven's

Door', made famous by Guns N' Roses. Both performances were top class, but Ruth's gutsy rendition clearly made an impact on the audience and they went wild for her when she came to the end of her last-ditch attempt to stay on the show. The decision was now down to the panel. Cheryl predictably chose Laura to stay on another week, but – sadly – the other judges thought Ruth had more fight left in her. A chorus of boos from the audience greeted the decision, as a very relieved Ruth dissolved into tears.

But it wasn't all bad news for Laura. That same week, the *X Factor* finalists' charity single 'Hero' topped the charts, knocking Girls Aloud's 'The Promise' off its number-one spot after it had been there just a week. Magnanimously, Cheryl said that she was happy that the contestants' song had usurped her single. 'It's for a good cause. I couldn't be happier for it to do well,' she commented to the *Sun*.

'The Promise' was Girls Aloud's first single from their fifth studio album, *Out of Control*. Released at the end of October, the song proved a massive hit with fans and critics alike. Sounding unlike anything they had released before, the Hi-NRG, sixties-influenced epic – backed by a stunning video clip, which saw the girls squeezed into body-hugging silver dresses and an array of sixties fashions – had smashed straight into the charts at number one the previous week, giving them their nineteenth top-ten hit. Cheryl and the rest of the band were thrilled.

As the autumn rushed by and the TV series continued, more of the talented wannabes were shot down in the public vote on *The X Factor*. Early favourites like Rachel Hylton were voted off the show while the likes of widower Daniel Evans, whom it seemed the judges disliked, remained for longer than expected. Yet of all the contestants fighting for their musical lives, it was young Diana Vickers, with her stunning looks and distinctive voice, who captured the public imagination. The press had found a sexy new star to splash across their pages, and predicted that she'd be the runaway winner.

But when Alexandra Burke performed Beyoncé Knowles's song 'Listen' the week before the semi-finals, the competition took a totally different turn. With a wind machine blowing her dress around her like she was already a true superstar on her own arena tour, Alexandra stunned the audience and the judges with a vocal so strong and defiant that the panel was left almost speechless. Louis said she was incredible, and branded her the 'best girl singer' in the competition. Dannii said that she deserved to be in the final, while Simon said she had made him proud to be British. 'You've really got to me,' the esteemed pop mogul revealed. 'Taking every performance from the show into consideration, that was – by far – the best perform-ance of the series.' Cheryl's confidence in her artists was now stronger than ever.

And justifiably so. Following the public vote, Cheryl mentored her two remaining contestants into the semi-final. 'I am proud of both of my girls. Reaching the semi-finals is a massive achievement,' she gushed on *The Xtra Factor*. 'Both my girls are terrified. There is a lot of pressure on Alexandra so she is more nervous. And Diana feels like she needs to step up. The reason why I have two acts is because they are so talented and so easy to work with. I just need to choose the right song. I have to be true to them.'

She added: 'The semis are such a hard place to be. You're one show away from the final, when it's out of everyone's hands.

Cos I have two girls, I'm guaranteed to have an act in the final ... and I will feel terribly ill when I get to the final.'

She was right, of course. She did get one act into the final. But it wasn't bookies' favourite Diana. Her versions of Avril Lavigne's 'Girlfriend' and Dido's 'White Flag' failed to woo the viewers, and – sensationally – she was voted off the show.

Cheryl was stunned by the shock cut, having believed that Diana had what it took to make it to the final. Nevertheless, she was still confident that the Blackburn lass had more to offer the world. 'I know people always say it,' she said on *The Xtra Factor*, 'but we haven't seen the last of her yet.'

Cheryl was, naturally, now fully behind Alexandra as they concentrated on the challenge that lay ahead. In Alex, Cheryl not only saw a singer desperate to succeed, but also a humble girl, one who wasn't in the least bit calculating. Now that Alex was through to the final, Cheryl was confident that, with her amazing vocals, there was nothing that could stop Alex from achieving her goal. Or was there?

The final episode of the series, on Saturday 13 December, was nothing short of spectacular. The three remaining acts – Cheryl's Alexandra, Simon Cowell's young Northern Irish singer Eoghan Quigg, and Louis's hunky boyband JLS – were to sing three songs each: a festive number, a duet with a surprise celebrity guest, and their favourite song from the series. After these performances, one finalist would be eliminated, after which two acts would battle it out to be crowned champion by performing what would become the winner's debut single: the Leonard Cohen classic 'Hallelujah', made famous in part by Jeff Buckley's 1994 cover version.

After their Christmas songs got everyone in the festive mood, tensions began to run high when JLS teamed up with

Westlife for a version of 'Flying Without Wings', and Eoghan was joined by Boyzone to sing their hit 'Picture Of You'. But neither performance had the emotional or show-stopping impact that Alexandra brought to the competition when she was joined on stage by her idol Beyoncé Knowles, to duet together on the song 'Listen'. The pair were sensational, and proved perfect vocal sparring partners. Although she was an amateur, Alexandra put up a fight and took on Beyoncé with the power and might of a woman who had been singing professionally for years.

It seemed clear, after Alexandra's amazing turn with the R&B legend, that the contest was pretty much over. Their rendition was certainly enough to get the audience and the judges jumping to their feet with appreciation. Even Beyoncé heaped praise on the London-born songstress and told her she was an incredible vocalist.

Unsurprisingly, Alexandra made it through to the final two, and was joined by JLS. After their respective versions of 'Hallelujah', a tearful Cheryl couldn't contain her emotions or her pride.

But there were more tears to come … when Alexandra was announced as the winner. Cheryl held her protégée's arm aloft like the champion she was. Afterwards, the triumphant mentor promised to stick by Alexandra and give her advice whenever she could. Her first suggestion was to keep men on the backburner while Alex concentrated on her first album.

Following the show, Cheryl exclaimed in a press conference: 'I am so proud of Alexandra. She is an amazing singer and I have every confidence that she will be a world-class star.'

Of course, while it was Alexandra who was named the *X Factor* winner, and who would go on to spend weeks at number one with her debut single, it was Cheryl who had stolen the series and captured the hearts of the nation. She was no longer just 'the fit one' from Girls Aloud. She was Cheryl Cole, a household name, and the woman who could seemingly do no wrong.

'She is Princess Cheryl,' former tabloid columnist Jessica Callan said on Channel 5's *The Cheryl Cole Factor*, a TV show celebrating the rise and rise of the *X Factor* judge. 'She is the nation's sweetheart. She can do no wrong – unless she had an affair with Simon Cowell.'

Of course, canoodling with her fellow judge was the furthest thing on Cheryl's mind – she had far more important things in hand.

Chapter 26
REACHING THE SUMMIT . . .

While Cheryl shone on *The X Factor*, Girls Aloud were caught up in the reflective glare. In fact, things couldn't have been going better for the girls. That autumn, their fifth studio album *Out of Control* hit the shops – and was met once again with universal praise. Very different-sounding from their previous work, some reviewers noted that the album didn't include any traditional Girls Aloud-type stompers, like 'Love Machine' or 'Wake Me Up'. Instead, the new collection featured a more laidback electro sound.

Among the stand-out tracks was 'The Loving Kind', a rather bittersweet dance tune, which had been penned by Xenomania and the Pet Shop Boys: a union that had had fans squealing with glee on Internet forums for months, ever since the collaboration was first announced. And the wait was worth it. The melody and lyrics were typically melancholy, while the girls' voices sounded more emotive than ever.

Working with the superstar pop duo, who were given a

Lifetime Achievement Award at the 2009 BRIT Awards, was an experience Cheryl confessed she'd never forget. 'Neil Tennant came in and taught me a harmony,' she told *Attitude* magazine, 'and I couldn't do it because I was so overawed. I always think of myself as a child in front of the telly singing "West End Girls".'

If she had been worried that Neil and his sidekick Chris Lowe would be scary Marys, though, she didn't have anything to fret about. They proved to be anything but intimidating divas. 'They are two of the nicest lads you could find,' Cheryl revealed to *Attitude*. 'Down to earth, lovely and genuine. Just nice lads to be around. I was going all blotchy red with my nerves and Brian [Higgins] told us they were nervous to meet us!'

Around the same time as the release of the album, in November, Girls Aloud published their first-ever official autobiography, *Dreams That Glitter: Our Story* (Bantam Press), in which Cheryl spoke for the first time about the heartache she had suffered during the Ashley-gate scandal. She confessed how she had sat in her house with the curtains closed, so that she could escape the paparazzi.

Yet she was also philosophical about the whole heartbreaking episode. 'People make mistakes, stuff happens,' she explained. She expressed her firm belief that every individual should be a free spirit, including her husband. 'I'm not his keeper. Ashley can have time with his friends when he wants, he can go out when he wants – of course he can. I'm not the type of person to ring him and be, like, "Where are you, who are you with, what's happening, what time will you be in, why haven't you answered your phone?"'

She went on to explain that she had experienced these

tough feelings before and was determined to learn from them. 'I've been that person in the past and I don't like it. I won't let anything change me and make me revert to being that type of girl, because it's not me.'

She also reasoned that marriage was a lifelong commitment – one that she didn't intend to shy away from – and that life was never meant to be easy; she was changing and learning all the time. 'When I said my wedding vows, I meant them,' she confided. 'I said them for life: for better, for worse. There's going to be worse times and better times. What's worth having anyway if it doesn't take a fight? Whatever happens, you learn another lesson. Things are sent to test you and I would hate to be an untested person.'

The book, in which she opened up about her childhood, when her mum could barely afford a can of beans, was another smash success, with a breakneck-paced ascent up the bestseller lists. Meanwhile, the girls celebrated Christmas with an ITV1 festive special, in which the group performed some of their biggest hits … and also got to flex their comic muscles in a series of hit-and-miss comedy sketches, alongside guest stars like Cilla Black, Paul O'Grady and Julie Goodyear. They duetted with credible chart stars – such as James Morrison, on a live performance of 'Broken Strings' – and even teamed up with their old 'pals' the Kaiser Chiefs.

The TV programme, broadcast on the same night as the *X Factor* final, rated over 8 million viewers and was in the top thirty of the most-watched shows of 2008. As the year came to an end, it was clear that, even after six years on the scene, Girls Aloud were still way ahead of the game, having seen off numerous rivals and gained the respect of their peers.

At the start of 2009, the band hit the ground running. They were over the moon when they discovered that they had been nominated in the Best British Group category at the BRIT Awards – and shortlisted for Best British Single for 'The Promise'. In addition, they had been invited by rock band Coldplay to join them at their summer shows at Wembley. The girls were finally being taken seriously – and they couldn't have been happier.

As always, though, there was a spoke in the wheel that managed momentarily to knock Cheryl off course.

At the end of 2008, Cheryl had taken part in a *Vogue* fashion spread, resulting in her gracing the cover of the style bible's February 2009 issue – a real honour, bearing in mind that she was the product of a reality show. Now, her profile, talent and stunning looks transcended those beginnings. When the magazine hit the shelves in the new year, the press had kittens about certain aspects of the interview that accompanied the gorgeous shots. For in it, she not only admitted that she used to cry about her weight in the early days of Girls Aloud – when she'd topped the scales at nine-and-a-half stone and therefore turned to the Atkins diet – but she also confessed that, when she was young, she was called 'P*ki' because she was small and dark and hairy.

What had the tabloid hacks and weekly mags really giddy, though, were the things she said about Victoria Beckham. In the world-exclusive interview, Cheryl hinted that she had been left deeply upset when her supposed best pal from the 2006 World Cup hadn't been in touch to lend a friendly shoulder to cry on during her bad time with Ashley – when even Coleen Rooney had offered support.

'I mean, David's mum is friends with Ashley's mum,' she told the esteemed magazine. 'Victoria was in my hotel room the whole time during the World Cup – we've had barbecues together – so I was quite shocked by that.'

Cheryl was misquoted by the press when she apparently told the *Guardian* that she would never wear any of Victoria's dress designs because they were for old people. It was left up to Kimberley Walsh to calm the waters. She explained that Cheryl had meant that the Beckham designs were more likely to be worn by sophisticated women, not necessarily young twenty-somethings.

Naturally, that didn't stop the press from whipping up an exaggerated story about how the WAG superstars were at loggerheads. But was there any truth in the rumours that the two A-listers were fighting like cat and dog?

Well, no – not according to an unnamed footballer's wife, and friend to both women, who told *OK!* magazine that there was no hint of a feud. In fact, both girls were apparently just as friendly as ever. The knowledgeable source also revealed how Victoria used to text Cheryl throughout *The X Factor* to say how well she was doing on the panel and how great she looked in her designer dresses. Fans were pleased to hear that the two most famous and successful WAGs were not warring after all.

January also saw the release of Girls Aloud's twentieth single, 'The Loving Kind', which disappointingly proved to be the band's lowest-charting single to date – although it was still a top-ten hit, at number ten. But just around the corner was a long-overdue achievement that would overshadow that. For although the girls lost out to Elbow in the category of Best British Group at the BRIT Awards ceremony on 18 February

2009, they were triumphant as artists of the Best British Single, 'The Promise'.

At last, they were content that they were established and totally accepted on the music scene (well, the voting public at least thought they deserved such a prestigious accolade). The girls were definitely here to stay. While rumours abounded that their *Out of Control* tour in the summer of 2009 would be their last, the band were adamant that they had no plans yet to split – and signed a three-album deal to prove it.

However, despite the news that they were planning on sticking around for some time to come, there were suggestions that future albums might include material produced by musicians *other* than Xenomania. For example, Coldplay had told the girls that they were trying to come up with the perfect song for them; and the band themselves spoke of collaborating with R&B stars like Ne-Yo.

The mooted plans had fans up in arms. They fretted that moving away from the producers who had given the girls so many hits, and who seemed to know exactly how they worked as a band, would harm the group in some way. After all, how many pop artists had actually survived once they felt they had matured enough to branch out with a new sound? The bargain bins are littered with the efforts of popstars who tried something new ... and ended up regretting their decision, big time. But with their record company keen to keep the hits coming, fans were assured that whatever the girls' new sound might be, it would be guaranteed to be a smash success.

Before the tour, and work on a sixth album, Cheryl embarked on her most physically arduous – and potentially dangerous – adventure to date.

In March 2009, Cheryl decided to climb Mount Kiliman-jaro. Not for fun, mind. She was doing it for a good cause. She and a bunch of kind-hearted celebs, including Gary Barlow, Kimberley Walsh, Alesha Dixon and Denise Van Outen, plotted to ascend the impressive mountain in Tanzania in aid of Comic Relief. She and the other celebrities took six months to prepare for the exhausting trek – but nonetheless, when they tackled it, the climb was harder than any of them thought it would be. Like so many challenges she had faced in the past, Cheryl approached it head-on, and raised more than a million pounds along the way.

That climb symbolizes her struggle to become successful. Cheryl Cole really has reached a peak in her career – and what a peak. She is on top of the world. Like a real-life Cinderella, all her dreams have miraculously come true.

Once upon a time, she was just a young girl who didn't know where the next meal was coming from and who had to wear her family's hand-me-downs. But she worked herself hard to make sure life had more to offer, and eventually she began to find success in a pop band, met and married her ideal man and, gradually, became the UK's princess of hearts. The journey wasn't always smooth, and she stumbled along the way, but she dealt with every hurdle with grace and dignity.

Cheryl no doubt still has lots more that she'd like to achieve. Although there are rumours that she wants to break America, either as a TV star or a solo artist, she's maintained throughout her marriage that all she really wants to do is start a family. So will Cheryl fulfil her dreams any time soon, once the summer tours are out of the way?

If she does, there's little doubt that she will embrace motherhood as successfully and as passionately as she has the rest of her life. The future seems to hold nothing but hope for the talented Cheryl Cole.

Index

Index